# Why Is God Always Late?

D1104176

**The Triune God is always gracious in the lives of His children, but have you noticed that His timing seems to be off? Or is it?**

**by the Rev. Dr. Curtis I. Crenshaw, Th.D.**

Footstool Publications
4008 Louetta Rd., Suite 542
Spring, TX 77388

Printed 2012

Why Is God Always Late?
ISBN: 978-1-877818-17-2

## My sites:

Dean of a seminary: www.CranmerHouse.org

Pastor of a church: www.SaintFrancisREC.org

Publisher: www.FootstoolPublications.com

Personal blog: curtiscrenshaw.wordpress.com

Sermons:

http://www.sermonaudio.com/source_detail.asp?sourceid=nicea325,

or go to www.SermonAudio.com and type in "St. Francis" (without the quotes).

# To William Dylan Smith

Faithful Husband to My Daughter

Godly Father to My Grandchildren

Lover of the Triune God

# Acknowledgements

My thanks to those who read this book for errors, not the least of whom was my wife Ruth, who also read it for accuracy, since she lived through most of these events with me. She has been by my side these 43 years, encouraging me, loving me, and believing in me.

Thanks also to Deaconess Teresa Johnson, a lifelong friend and servant of Christ in His Church. She has a razor-sharp eye that catches just about everything, and is a technical writer as well as writer of poetry (http://angliverse.wordpress.com/). Of course, any remaining errors are mine.

Another lifelong friend, David Potts, designed the cover of this book, and I hope the reader will find it attractive. In my humble opinion, he is talented, not only with computers, but also with design.

# Contents

# How Did This Book Happen?

**W**hy is God Always Late?" Over the past 40 years I've preached sermons with the title of this book, and I've talked to many people about the various trials I've experienced over the decades. The title (*Why Is God Always Late?*) is meant to be provocative; obviously, God is never later.

Recently, several of those people suggested that I write a memoir before I get too old to remember these accounts of God's faithfulness. They believed these stories would be an encouragement to others, and my wife Ruth enthusiastically agreed. Thus, this book is about God's tendency to wait until the last minute to rescue me (and you). And since this is a record of God's faithfulness in my life, please pardon the many times I've used the first person ("I").

This story is true to the best of my memory, but when my memory is unclear, I will refer to the diary I kept during several periods of my life. I will state whether I'm quoting my diary or my memory. Of course, some who have been involved with me in the past will find fault with my memory in a few details; so be it. Only the Triune God is omniscient. But a good friend of mine recently said of my detailed memory of the past, "Either you're lying or you have an extraordinary memory for details. Either way I can't tell, for even though I was there for some of those events, I can't remember them except in broad strokes."

God has enabled me to recall distant details. Once I recalled a man's name that we had met in a crucial time, who was the first diamond grader in the South, and the company he worked for. When I compared my notes written 31 years ago and not read since, I was right, even down to the month and year we went to see him. I can recall the time I bowled an 800 series, where I was (Cherokee Lanes in Memphis, TN), what the lane numbers were (25-26), when (fall of 1966, late at night) and against whom (Richard). From 1966 I can recall who the general manager of the lanes was (Chester Morgandale), the day time manager (Charlie Edgin), the nighttime manager (Ralph Abernathy), and even the mechanic who kept the bowling machines going (Danny Carver). I remember the man who was my best-ball partner in late night bowling (David Pauly), and that several times we bowled a 300, together, that is, not individually. I can recall every major event in my life to the month and year, and sometimes to the day. My wife says I clutter my mind with such trivia, but I don't try to retain such; it is just there. But I can't recall where I put my coffee cup two minutes ago or who called me last week!

When I have used real names, I've not used quotes, but the actual names. But to protect others, I have sometimes used pseudonames, which always have quotes around them, such as "Hugh." It is not my purpose to prosecute anyone, but to demonstrate how the Lord Christ has guided my life with His timing miracles.

This memoir does not cover every aspect of my life but mostly the trials I've had, enough of each trial to see the message of the book, which is God's miraculous timing in mine and Ruth's life. Usually I give details leading up to a trial so His timing can be appreciated and savored all the more.

Regarding my sins, I have plenty to mention and could entertain the reader with them, but it would not be profitable for me or edifying for the reader. Though some of them have to be named, the point of the book is not me but Him. I truly hope that you'll see His hand of deliverance in my life and His miraculous timing. The first few pages are background that is necessary for the rest of the book. Therefore, be sure to **read the next chapter**.

# What Is This Book About?
# (please read this)

**Y**ou may be hurting too much even to consider a book like this, but do you want help? Do you need someone to understand how far away God seems sometimes, and why He's so slow to get things done? If so, this book is for you.

I was in the infantry and survived the Tet Offensive in Vietnam while many of my friends did not survive, or were injured seriously. I patched up my fellow infantry men and had them rescued by helicopter and taken to safety. "You surely were *lucky*," a friend once said to me. I always cringe when someone uses the word "luck," for that presupposes a god of chaos. No, my survival in Vietnam was not due to my superior planning (there wasn't any!), or my alleged robust and dogged character (what is that?). I was preserved by God's gracious timing.

As I look back over my 67 years, I've had a major trial every decade of my life, and some in between, and it usually seemed that God's timing was terrible, until time had passed, and I looked back. Then things seemed very different, even gracious.

By "God," I mean the Triune God, the Father and the Son and the Holy Spirit, not the generic God that politicians often invoke when they say "*God* bless you" which sounds religious and allows their hearers to fill in the blank about "God's" identity.

There is no generic God but only the Triune God, Who providentially reigns over all creation. But what is "Providence"? This is the only time I'll use a technical word in this book, but providence is that mysterious working of God in making all things turn out good, in the long run, for His people:

> And we know that all things work together for good to those who love God, to those who are the called according to His purpose (Rom. 8:28).

Carefully note that this verse does not say that everything is good, or that each isolated thing is good but that over time, "all things work *together* for good." "Together" includes other things. For example, a minor car wreck would be bad, but if we add that it kept us from being hit head on by an eighteen-wheeler, then it was good.

But what is "good"? That is defined as what God does to minister grace to us to make us conform to the moral image of His Son, Jesus Christ (Rom. 8:29).

I cannot interpret God's providence with certainty, for it is a mystery, and I especially do not try to use past providence to predict the particulars of future providence. I can only look back with humility and be grateful to the One who loved me and gave Himself for me, and thus has guided my life by His mysterious sovereignty. I have studied God's sovereignty theoretically for decades, taught it in seminary, written about it, but this book is the practical side of that mystery. Indeed, He *makes* me live it, whether I want to or not! If I had my way, I would be a billionaire, famous, and have a dozen homes in various parts of the world. Instead, He has met my needs ("This day, my daily bread"), given me ministry as pastor in churches and as dean of a seminary, while providing me with a comfortable home. Moreover, I have a wonderful wife of 43 years and counting, two godly children, each of whom has a Christian spouse and two godly children. But the greatest gift I have is the Lord Jesus Christ. It is from Him that all other gifts flow, and with Him, I must be satisfied.

Is this book about miracles? Does the Triune God do miracles today? Well, He is God, so what would we expect? Yet He rarely does the kind of miracle that we see Jesus doing when He healed someone instantly, perfectly, and with just the spoken word, though surely He can and probably does that on occasion. That being true, we cannot manipulate Him with our "faith" and demand that He spring from a bottle like a genie to grant us our wishes. Faith and prayer are designed to help us submit to God, not to control Him. One major assumption of this book, though rarely stated explicitly, is that we are not in charge of our lives—He is. Thus the timing of events is what **He** does, not what we do. Too often people in our churches today assume that worship is about them so they engage in entertainment, grand standing, thinking they can control God if they can conjure enough faith. We are His servants, not the reverse.

The "miracles" God does today, and has done in my life, are primarily "miracles" of timing, bringing people and circumstances together in such a way that trials suddenly evaporate, and if not suddenly, then over time work out in such an unusual manner that the only explanation is the providence of our sovereign Creator, the Father and the Son and the Holy Spirit. My responsibility is to have patience and to use human means of grace to work things out.

Let us consider something about time, since this book is about God's timing in my life. Whatever time is, it has been created by God. We as creatures will never be outside time; that is the Triune God's domain, the realm of eternity, where time neither begins nor ends. For us it has a beginning but not an end. All the lives of all creatures on earth are governed by God's created time. For example, the earth rotates to give us 24 hours. The moon orbits the earth to give us months. The earth orbits the sun to give us years. The seven day week is revealed by God in Genesis one.

Time is also the past. As a tree without roots produces no fruit, a person without a past is barren, because he does not know who he is or where he is going. Without a past, we are just dandelions, blown about by the whims of a godless culture (Psalm 1:4; Eph. 4:14).

Moreover, in Galatians 4:4 we read:

> When the fullness of the time had come, God sent
> forth His Son, born of a woman, born under the law.

God subjected His Son to time, having planned just the right moment for Him to enter the world, which means that every detail of His life had meaning, which in turn implies every detail of our lives has meaning. Every moment of our lives has everlasting potential, for everything we do will either be confirmed or denied at the Last Day judgment. Moreover, we all have the same amount of time, 24 hours a day, seven days a week, 52 weeks a year. No one, no matter how rich or how powerful, can add another minute to this plan. But we can use His time wisely by living for Him or foolishly by storing up toys to leave to others. The choice is ours—and His—as you will see.

Finally, as the children of Israel were about to enter the Promised Land, having spent 40 years in the wilderness, here is what Moses said to them:

> "And you shall remember that the LORD your God
> led you all the way these forty years in the wilderness,
> to humble you *and* test you, to know what was in your
> heart, whether you would keep His commandments or
> not. So He humbled you, allowed you to hunger, and fed
> you with manna which you did not know nor did your fa-
> thers know, that He might make you know that man

shall not live by bread alone; but man lives by every
word that proceeds from the mouth of the LORD" (Deut.
8:2-3).

In other words, life is not about being happy but about being
holy, not about the collection of things but about maturity in one's
walk with the Triune God.

Now let us take the adventure of seeing a charmed life, for I
have lived with a sovereign wall around me (a hedge, as Satan said in
Job 1:10), and nothing can happen without His will.

# Chapter 1: Murder My Mother?

The bat was flying through the duplex at night from room to room with my mother (Frances) and me squealing, pulling the cover over our heads, and her brother, my Uncle Jim, trying to catch it. He finally chased it out an open window. The year was 1949; I was four, but I recall that incident clearly, and Uncle Jim confirmed the details recently (July 2012).

My grandmother Mee-Maw, my grandfather, Pee-Paw, mother (Frances), and my Uncle Jim and I lived on one side of the duplex, and my grandmother's brother and his family on the other side.

I also recall almost being hit by a pickup truck when we lived at the duplex. The driver slammed his brakes, barely missed me, grabbed me by the arm, and took me to Mee-Maw. The driver said that something moved me out of the way, or I would have been hit for sure. Mee-Maw would later say it was an angel.

At night, my uncle would shoot large rats in the back yard with a .22, in the city, using very small bullets called CB Caps. That neighborhood in Memphis, TN was so poor and run down that the city tore it down completely a few years after we moved from there (we moved in 1949), and even bulldozed the streets and renamed them. We lived on Peyton at the time.

Once, Mee-Maw and Mother gave me a fuzzy monkey they called Jeepers, which I kept until I was grown. I slept with it as a small boy. When I was four, we moved to Vinton St. in Memphis, and lived there one year. Mee-Maw's sister, Aunt Blanch, lived around the corner, and I can recall playing in the water at the curb after a sudden rain. Then at age five we moved to 892 Philadelphia, Memphis, one block from the fairgrounds. My memory comes alive during the six years we lived there.

Again, it was a duplex. Each side was long and narrow like a 600 square foot cracker box that went straight back from the front door. The first room was the living room where Mother slept. The next room was the only bedroom where Mee-Maw and Pee-Paw slept. Then there was a small bath; no shower in those days. Next was a small kitchen with a stove, and a small refrigerator with ice in metal trays that we had to beat out with a small hammer. Mee-Maw did our laundry on a rub board, and later upgraded to a washer with a mechanical arm that would squeeze the water out of the clothes between two rollers. She was really proud of that! Off the kitchen was a pantry area that we turned into a bedroom for my uncle and me. There was not enough room for two horizontal beds so we slept on bunk beds. This duplex is still there.

My mother came to faith in Christ about the time I was born, and my father left us about two years later, after he had returned from WWII. I don't remember him from that time. One often sees in movies a son hating his father because he was abandoned as a small child, but I never experienced that. I was 14 the first time my dad took me anywhere (fishing on Horseshoe Lake in Arkansas, and we got into a terrible wasp nest!), and there were only three other occasions that he spent any time with me. Uncle Jim, who is still living, became my surrogate father, and as a Christian he influenced me greatly. We hunted, watched *Have Gun Will Travel* and *Gunsmoke*, went shooting, and just hung out together. In many ways I was like a big brother to his children, my cousins, Mike and Shirley. (Pam came along later.) When changing their diapers interfered with watching the two shows just mentioned, I complained: "I'm never going to get married, and if

I do something that stupid, I'm never having kids." Those words tasted good when I had to eat them. The Lord had removed my dad from my life and replaced him with Uncle Jim. To this day (1 August 2012), we still have wonderful fellowship in the Lord.

My father remarried and told his new wife that I was not his child, but that mother had me outside marriage (adultery). He denied this lie when he was with me. His mother ("Shussie," pronounced "Shuh-she"), never forgave him for that lie. As I grew up, I looked like him, so he never wanted us to be in the same room with his second wife, and I was never allowed in his home. I talked to him about the Lord the last year of his life, but he had all the answers. My heart grieved for him as I watched him die in a coma, outside Christ, from cirrhosis of the liver; he had drunk himself to death. I was there primarily to support his daughter, my half sister, whose mother died that same week independent of him with Alzheimer's in a nursing home. She received a double blow in one week.

After we moved to Philadelphia Street when I was five, **one of the most significant things in my life occurred that is still very much part of me**. Mother and Mee-Maw started me memorizing the Bible from the old King James Version, which was about the only version freely available in those days. I recall how excited I was when the first memory book came in. It was a planned program called BMA, Bible Memory Association. We memorized 15 to 20 verses *per week*, and were only allowed a few errors, and the results had to be reported to an official person. As I progressed, I would get awards, usually a Christian book of some kind, or a Bible, and I still have those awards. If I completed the whole program, I could get a free week at camp. I did not take advantage of those free weeks until I was older. Once when I went, the boys made fun of my legs, which seem to connect under my arm pits, but they stopped laughing when they saw me run. I had no equal in grade school or junior high school at 40 yards, and only one boy could beat me at 100 yards.

If you caught my age, I had not begun school yet when I began to memorize Scripture and so could not read, but that did not bother mother or Mee-Maw! I did not know any better so I memorized what they told me, and I still recall many of those verses and often quote them as I teach and preach. Later, when I became a teenager, I tried varied excuses to get out of memorizing, but Mom was very godly (still is!), and did not listen to my antics. It was memorize or stay home so I memorized.

In 1951, I began grammar school at age six in the first grade at Peabody Elementary School, and at first was taken to school by mother, but quickly began to walk the mile and later rode a bike. I have good memories of those years.

## Mom Marries Again

After a few years, my mother began to date some Christian men. She was beautiful, and could have been competitive with any Miss America, and I'm sure many of them wanted to marry her. Somehow she met a Southern Baptist preacher from Paducah, KY, named Rudy. He had twins by a previous marriage, Letha Nell and Lennis Dale, both of whom are now dead. Mother trusted him and thus did not investigate his first marriage.

While I was in the sixth grade at Peabody, they got married, and I attended the wedding. Dr. Robert G. Lee performed the wedding at Bellevue Baptist Church. I was eleven, and after a month or two, they had me come to live with them at 2511 Cantor Ave, which also does not exist anymore. (I guess I have a knack for closing down neighborhoods!) For the first time, we had a car, a TV, and even a window air conditioning unit, and the single family house had two bedrooms and about 800 square feet! We were really living well!

Rudy's daughter had married at 15 so she stayed in Paducah, but her brother Lennis came to live with us. We shared a bedroom. It stroked my ego to have a step-father who was the pastor of the church we attended and to have the new appliances, except that we dried the clothes on a clothes line in the back yard, and when it was cold, the clothes froze. I felt better about life.

My step brother and I got along well enough, but not great. He cared nothing about the things of the Lord, and I wondered how a preacher's son could be so calloused. He was about four years older than me. He smoked, though he was not supposed to, and I was always hiding his cigarettes from him, or putting water on them. Once I put dog's hairs in a number of them, and he could not figure out why they tasted so bad. I never did tell him. Of course, he was always chasing me, and when Mom and "Dad" were gone, he would make me do weird things, like any time I wanted to move around the house I had to hop on one foot. Then there were the frogs on the arms he would give me, but I guess that was just boy stuff.

## Divorce Already?

After mom had been married two years to the preacher, she took me for a long walk. She seemed very serious, but she did not cry, telling me that she and Rudy would divorce. I knew he was not much of a dad to me, but things did not seem that bad. "Why?" I asked. I was almost fourteen.

She said, "You know "Helen" in the church?" to which I nodded yes. Her husband had been killed in a car wreck, leaving her with several children but also with a large life insurance policy, double indemnity for accidental death.

She continued, "Rudy has been seeing her, and I think they are having physical relations. Anyway, he says he wants a divorce."

To make matters worse, mom was seven months pregnant. I was stunned. How could anyone, especially a Christian pastor, be so cold to want to leave his pregnant wife, step-son, and his unborn child? What would he say to his son? Or to his daughter? As a preacher, What would he tell his congregation? "Helen" only lived a few blocks away, so one day Mother and I drove close to the house. I jumped out, sneaked up to the window, and there was Rudy sitting close to her. I wanted to kick his teeth in, but I wasn't big enough.

If mother had checked into Rudy's background, she would have discovered that he was divorced because he got in trouble with a very young girl in Paducah, and had to leave in a hurry, abandoning his church. He came to Memphis, and being a very suave and cunning man, got another Southern Baptist church. He loved sex almost as much as money, but what would he do to keep his church and marry another person in the church?

He concocted a plan that would have made Machiavelli proud. He would give Mother an overdose of some kind of medication, say that she was depressed and took it herself, wait for it to take effect, then slowly drive her to the hospital. He knew the medication she was taking was lethal in large doses. That way he could seem to be the pious and loving husband, taking his wife and unborn child to the hospital, but it would be too late. The plan worked quite well at first. Mother was about seven months pregnant when Rudy administered the pills. She was already in a very depressed state, and was under the influence of some other medication. She did not know what she was doing in taking the medication Rudy gave her, though later she would remember what he had done. I was not there, but Mee-Maw was taking care of mother who was having a difficult pregnancy.

After some time had passed, he calmly walked into Mee-Maw's bedroom, which was mine also, and calmly said, "Frances has taken an overdose and is unconscious. We need to take her to the hospital."

He did not want to call emergency (911 did not begin until 1968 and this was 1958) because they would get her to the hospital quickly and pump her stomach, so he piously volunteered to drive her to the hospital. In 1958, all the hospitals were in downtown Memphis, and we lived way out by the airport, about twelve miles away. He carried mother to the car unconscious (she was 5 feet two, and he was well over six feet), and drove carefully to make sure he hit the traffic lights on red.

## The Timed Wreck

**Here is where God's timing is miraculous**. After only a short distance from the house, he had a minor wreck. Mee-Maw, who was in the back seat with mother, was beside herself. She jumped out, grabbed some passer-by and said: "My daughter is pregnant and unconscious from an overdose of pills. Can you please rush us to the hospital?"

The passer-by quickly grabbed Mother, threw her in his car with Mee-Maw, and they went racing to the hospital, blowing the horn and running traffic lights. Rudy stayed behind to take care of the wreck. The emergency room took her immediately, pumped her stomach, and saved hers and the baby's life. Rudy was thrown out of the house, but how could anything be proved? Mother had taken the pills, had a vague remembrance of it, and it would be her word against his.

The deacons of the Baptist church wanted to take Rudy for a "ride," not to kill him, but to make him wish he were dead. As I listened from another room, Mother talked them out of it. That kind of thing happened in those days, and the police would have looked the other way. Mother's divorce attorney would later say that Rudy had the coldest heart of anyone he had dealt with in his entire legal practice, and he was an older man with decades of experience.

**Not only did God's timing with the car wreck save mother's life, it also saved my little brother**, Paul. We have been close all our lives. During mother's pregnancy, I would run around the house singing, "I want a baby brother, I want a baby brother" and God honored that desire. Of course, in those days you did not know a baby's gender until birth.

Even after all that, Mother was willing to forgive Rudy, but he moved to Dallas with "Helen," and tried to get another Baptist church but the deacons at Brooks Road Baptist Church in Memphis put a stop to that, so he went into real estate, quickly going through "Helen's" money.

Paul was born on December 24th, 1958, and I turned 14 two months later. Mother entered the most difficult part of her life: taking care of a teen and a baby while working full time. Compound those difficulties with feelings of rejection, and it was even worse, if possible. (I have the best mom ever!) Rudy went to Texas because, at that time, the alimony and child support laws were very liberal, favoring the man. It took quite some time, but eventually he had to pay up. Thirteen years later I would be in Dallas attending seminary, and Paul would be living with my wife Ruth and me. Rudy came *one* time to see Paul, asking questions for information to get out of paying child support; it did not work.

Rudy and his two children are now dead. I think his daughter became a Christian later in life, and though married at 15, she and her husband stayed together until her untimely death from a disease. I don't know what happened to Lennis, only that he married after going to Dallas with his father. Rudy eventually got another church in the Winsboro, TX area. Recently, my beloved mother called "Helen" to see how she was doing and to tell her that she had long ago forgiven her. "Helen" was taken aback by such graciousness.

On January 1st at 12:05 A.M., 1983, I presided over the wedding of Mother to her current husband, Barry Gillespie, a godly man who loves her. Third time is charm, they say, and this has been a good marriage. I also presided over their 25th anniversary when they renewed their vows.

As I look back on that experience, **I can see the hand of the Lord and His timing**, especially with the wreck. Why He allowed mother to marry such a scoundrel is a mystery. Of course, we have our own wills. Looking at it from man's perspective, the whole thing could have been avoided if mother had checked Rudy's background, but who would have thought of that? God allows us to go a long way before He pulls us back. He allows the wicked schemes of people seemingly to have their way (Psalm 73), and for a time our lives are miserable, but in the end He judges those who do not repent, and He blesses His faithful people.

I've also learned that *without pain, we do not gain* in the Christian life but merrily go our way, loving our sins, and not changing. If there is anything I hope I've learned, it is that He'll let us have enough rope to trip ourselves up but not enough to hang ourselves. Then He comes in to clean up our mess. Now I date myself, but do you recall the Laurel and Hardy movies? They nearly always ended with Hardy saying to Laurel in that disgusted manner, looking straight at the camera: "Well, here's another fine mess you've gotten me into." That is what we do to ourselves when we do not apply biblical teaching to our lives—going to church, singing hymns, listening to the preacher, and then going home, where nothing changes. We make bad decisions and get ourselves into a mess. Then we dismiss it by saying, "That's just one of those things." Right, God wasn't in it, we think. We may not be theoretical atheists, but sometimes we are practical atheists. God has to get our attention. Sometimes our loving God lets us mess things up to teach us lessons we would not learn otherwise.

My mother was an excellent disciplinarian. She would take the Bible, read to me what I had done wrong, tell me what was right, then administer the belt of education to the seat of knowledge to "encourage" me to do better. I'm reminded of this passage where God does the same with His children:

> And you have forgotten the exhortation which speaks to you as to sons: "My son, do not despise the chastening of the LORD, **Nor be discouraged when you are rebuked by Him**; For whom the LORD loves He chastens, **And scourges <u>every</u> son whom He receives.**" If you endure chastening, God deals with you as with sons; for what son is there whom a father does not chasten? But if you are without chastening, of which all have become partakers, then you are illegitimate and not sons (Hebrews 12:5-8).

In his excellent book, *Where Is God When It Hurts*, Philip Yancey tells of a medical doctor who has done much research of leprosy patients. The disease is not the problem so much as what it does; it deadens the nerves to pain so that one does not feel anything. Patients accidently hit themselves on something, burn themselves on a stove, break a limb, and are not even aware they have been injured. Over time, the injury will bleed internally or get infected, and that is often what kills them. He and a team devised a wire mesh to fit over the patients so that when they did something to themselves, there would be a loud buzz in their ear. The buzz was annoying so the people either took the mesh off or turned off the buzzer. It was then that the good doctor realized that pain was a gift from God **to make** us change. So it is with trials and God's timing. He makes us sweat, allows extreme emotional pain, such as financial loss or the loss of a loved one, and once He has our attention, we begin to grow again in our relationship with Him. He wants holiness; we want toys and ease. He *will* get His way so we had better do His will voluntarily.

Through the near loss of my dear mother and my brother, I learned not to take life for granted. Through that **miraculous car wreck at the last minute**, I learned that even when all seems lost, God's timing is always perfect. By the way, I never heard my mother complain against the Lord God through any of this.

# Chapter 2: The Bowling god

When I graduated from Central High School in 1963, I was happy and content. I had been admitted to a prestigious private Roman Catholic engineering college, but I was admitted on probation as my grades were mixed in high school. I did well in what I liked, and badly in what I hated. I liked math, science, radio classes, biology, and hated English, history, and Civics. So I thought electrical engineering would be good for me. My paternal grandmother had saved all my life for me to go to college, as no one in my family had a college degree. I would be the first.

Over the summer I taught myself trigonometry and how to use a slide ruler, both with books from the public library. I was excited to enter the college in September of that year, but after only two months, President Kennedy was assassinated in Dallas (November 1963), which put a cloud over the whole campus for some time. I recall where I was and what I was doing when I heard the dreadful news, not believing it at first.

Once again old habits would die hard. As the fall semester progressed, I found myself doing well in courses I liked and muddling in courses I hated. Then I found something I loved more than anything—bowling. I became obsessed with it. (After I married, years later my wife would say that I can never do anything in moderation. She is probably right.) I searched all the major libraries in the city and checked out books explaining the physics and techniques of bowling. I got a job at the largest bowling center in the city, Cherokee Lanes, 52 lanes all in a row, coached little league, joined a men's bowling league, and joined the college bowling team. With all those activities,

I could bowl free as many games as I wanted, usually about 24 hours per week. I got good at it. I had secret desires to become a pro, but intellectually I knew that was about as probable as catching a bullet with my teeth. Desires overruled my mind, and my grades suffered more than ever as I often bowled all night on weekends, and during the week. (I still understand the physics and like to watch the pros on TV.)

After about three years of college and two years of bowling (mother knew only a little of the latter), my mother suggested that I take a year off from engineering and attend one year at the local Bible college to receive a theological foundation for life. After calculus and differential equations, I thought Bible college would be a glorified Sunday School class—wrong! They talked of the hypostatic union, of various views of original sin (such as traducianism, creationism, and so forth), and of predestination, which made me mad. Surely God would not predestine things, would He? What about my "free will"? (Later, I would appreciate such verses as Acts 4:26-28 where the wicked acts of Israel and the Gentiles at the cross accomplished, without coercion, what God had predestined to occur.)

Then one day after class, the man whom I later came to consider my favorite professor of all time (and I've had 11 years of school after high school), Paul Moody Davidson, reprimanded me. (D. L. Moody was Davidson's grand uncle. Dr. Paul Davidson helped my mother greatly through the "Rudy" trial so she named my brother "Paul David.") He vehemently scolded me for staying out late bowling and not being ready for class, which told me that mother had talked with him. I made three F's that one semester. Later, after I learned some valuable lessons in Vietnam and returned from the Army to attend full time, I was given the academic award in my graduating class.

# Chapter 3: I Have to Go Where?

It was October of 1966 when I received the letter. It was completely unexpected. It said:

> Greeting:
> You are hereby ordered for induction into the
> Armed Forces of the United States, and to report at 767
> Federal Office, Bldg., 167 N. Main St., Memphis, Tenn,
> on November 9, 1966 at 6:45 A.M.

(I still have that letter!) Not only was this a shock that petrified me, but I was to report at "6:45 A.M.," which jolted me as badly as my grandfather's rooster when his comb hit the electric fence one dewy morning, scattering feathers everywhere. I stared at the letter in disbelief. "Surely this is some mistake, Lord. If it's a joke, I'm not laughing."

I mulled over the words, "Greeting," not "Dear Curtis," or "Dear Mr. Crenshaw," and there was no explanation—just a command, "*You are hereby ordered for induction.*" It was "Greeting," singular, not "Greetings," and to this day I hate that word, "Greeting." When I hear that word, it is like fingernails on a chalk board. Arrgghh. I was beginning to understand what W. C. Fields once said: "Start every day with a smile and get it over with."

I read the letter several times, and my stomach felt as though I was falling from some high altitude. I received the letter in the afternoon when I returned home from classes at the Bible college, and my mind took over, detailing the worst, playing "what if" until I was numb with fear, anger, and thoughts of death. Conflict in Vietnam was hot (1966), and all I could think about was the worst possible outcome.

My mother's brother, Thomas, who was looking forward to seeing me after WWII and wrote about his sister giving him a nephew or niece, never made it home. He was killed in February 1945, the month I was born, and never knew my gender. Mee-Maw said the Lord took one and gave her another one the same month. I could see a repeat with my little brother taking my place. The rest of that day and for several weeks thereafter, I was dominated with thoughts of Vietnam. I went bowling.

I could not sleep, my mind would not shut off as I wondered if I would pass the physical, and could think of no reason I would not. I plotted what I could do to fail it. I contemplated breaking a leg or something. Maybe I could have a minor car wreck. At the physical, they lined us against the wall like a firing squad. After all the tests, the M.D. at the end said I was in perfect condition. "Lord, couldn't I at least have a hemorrhoid?"

Then I tried to get into the Army Medic Reserve, passed another physical, but it was too late. If I had applied before the draft notice, I would have been accepted. **In this case, God's timing said No**.

Mee-Maw, unknown to me, called the President's (USA) office to get me excused, saying that her son had been killed in WWII. A secretary called her to explain that I was not exempt. I went to my Bible college to find out why my student deferment did not keep me out of the draft, but discovered that changing majors had made me eligible. Nothing that I tried worked—"Anything, just get me out of this, O Lord! This can't be happening."

**It was then I discovered something of God's sovereignty and timing**. He could shut doors, bring things together in such a way that it seemed I was in a corridor. All doors were locked but one, and I could not stay in the corridor. The law required me to walk through that one door to the Army. I was foaming inside, and I did not like what I saw in myself. I had always heard that what is down in the well comes up in the bucket. Rebellion was coming up.

I never heard of going to Canada, but would not have done so anyway. It was not that I did not love my country, but it seemed that I was being taken away when I had the best part of college to go. I was angry at the government for wanting to waste my life, and maybe take it from me, permanently. At first I could not believe God was in it, for He would not treat me like this, would He? Like a dog that snaps at the rock and not the one who threw it, I only saw the immediate circumstances, not the loving Lord behind them. At the time, my theology would not allow that God could work through bad circumstances; that was the devil's work. So I fretted day and night.

Meanwhile, my best friend, Richard, who was a robust six feet, very athletic, strong, and healthy man, had about three times my strength. He had also received a draft letter. He was not in college so I thought he would be taken almost immediately. But when he returned from his medical exam, he was beaming and said:

"Guess what?"

I said, "When do you leave?"

He responded, "Here is what the doctor said at the end of the exam. 'Mr. Woodward, you are permanently disqualified from military service because you have a bad hernia. Go to your civilian doctor as soon as possible to get it taken care of before it gets worse.'"

"Well, did you?"

"My doctor examined me, and said, 'Hernia, what hernia'?"

I looked at him in disbelief; there went my stomach again. Now I was *really* upset. That was 1966, and he has never had hernia problems to this day. Though I was also athletic, I was smaller, not nearly as strong, and yet they wanted me and not him to carry an 80 pound pack! "Come on, Lord, what is this? Surely, You jest!"

I wondered what life would be like in my family if I were killed in Vietnam, and I stressed over my little brother, 14 years younger than I. Who would look after him? He had already had enough stress when his father, my step-father, abandoned him. He did not need to lose another loved one. Did not the Lord know this? "**What terrible timing, Lord Jesus**."

What if I were maimed for life? Who would take care of me? I did not want to be a burden to others. Moreover, though I had grown up hunting in the woods, I did not want to live in the jungle for a year fighting human enemies, not to mention spiders, mosquitoes, and highly poisonous snakes I did not recognize. I had played with snakes, scorpions, black widows, and bees of all kinds while growing up, but I knew the USA critters. Besides, I hate mosquitoes, but they love me!

When a door is shut, and nothing I do makes any difference, the Lord is in it. He has something planned for me that is good, even though I don't think so. When things go "bad" and nothing changes it, even though someone has sinned against me and I don't seem to deserve what is happening, God is in it. Then again I may have brought it on myself with my own sin or with stupidity, but God will still use it in my life, in the long run. I must resign myself to rest in Him, for I can be sure that no amount of squirming, frustration, foaming, anger, complaining, or agitation will change God's mind. At this point in my life, I am more conscious than ever of His majesty, sovereignty, and on the other side of the trial, I'll see that He was working things out for good.

## Going Away Party

My mother knew I was going bowling with my best friend, David, and she suggested that I wear a tie.

"Mom, we're just going bowling, not to church."

"But you would look so nice."

"Nice for whom, the pins? I would sweat all night."

My best friend from the first grade, David Merriman (who died in 2008 from injuries received in a car wreck), organized a surprise going away party for me to the Army. He had served four years in the Air Force. He told me we were going bowling, but that he needed to stop by the Bible college for a minute to see his girl friend, Rebecca. That sounded reasonable to me, but then he asked me to go in with him. I did not see the need for that, but after his prodding, I went. Then he proceeded down stairs, and I heard him rattling a soft drink machine. He said, "Curt, come down here to see if you can get this thing to give me a coke."

As I descended the stairs, I noticed that the lights were out. Students of the opposite sex were not allowed in the dark together at the Bible college in 1967, and I wondered if Dave were kissing his girlfriend, which was definitely not allowed. I said to myself, "What in the world," and about that time all the lights came on, and everyone jumped out and yelled "Surprise!" I could not believe it. They had planned a party just for me, and it was the most surprised I've ever been. Mother was there with a tie that she had offered me earlier.

# Chapter 4: Military Training

## Basic Training

I resigned myself to go to the Army, but it seemed to be **terrible timing** to interrupt my college, take me from my little brother, and expose me to injury or death. I silently asked, "What is the point, Lord?"

In February 1967, my paternal step-grandfather, Cecil, who had served many years in the military, took me to the Federal building in downtown Memphis, dropped me off with tears in his eyes and said: "I served 12 years in the military so listen to me. Do what you're told; don't volunteer for anything; and keep your mouth shut." That proved to be excellent advice. I was 21.

We had about two weeks of orientation before basic training began where they gave us a slew of written tests, taught us about military law, and how to march. I had had two years of ROTC in high school and knew how to march and drill with a rifle, which landed me a squad leader position—I tried to get out of it but could not, though I managed to avoid being a platoon leader.

On one occasion we were taken four at a time into a room where there were four military barbers. One of the barbers asked a cadet in his chair how he wanted his hair cut, and the rest of us just watched. The naïve guy proceeded to tell him about how long he wanted it on the sides, just off the ears, and how long on the top. The barber said, "You got it," and he buzzed him right down the middle! The cadet's eyes bulged while everyone else laughed, and all the barbers buzzed us in unison.

Days later, when they were ready for us to begin basic training, they awakened us early, and we had assembly line shots in both arms as we walked between two rows of Army medics. At one point they put an air gun on each shoulder and said, "Don't move." They counted together and I got two shots at once, along with many needle shots as I progressed between the medics. Once our arms and bottoms were loaded, they drove us to the basic training area. Our very nice Sgt. Deriso (I still clearly remember his name and I have our basic training album) turned from Dr. Jekyll to Mr. Hyde. He began screaming at us to get off the bus, and I mean *screaming*. I could not believe it because he had been so nice during the days of orientation. We had duffle bags full of items they had given us, and we had to ship home everything we had, including dirty underwear. I was only allowed to keep my KJV Bible.

As we exited the bus, there were other sergeants screaming orders at us to drop to the ground to do pushups, with arms full of shots, no less. My grandfather had explained it to me so I was at least prepared that it would happen, but just shocked at the timing. After another period of harassment, another sergeant yelled, "Are you tired, trainees?" Without thinking, we responded: "NO, SERGEANT." He screamed, "Good, do pushups." Another sergeant shouted after we had done pushups for quite a while, "Are you tired, trainees?" We thought we had him this time: "Yes, sergeant." He yelled, "I can't HEAR you." We yelled back, "YES, SERGEANT." He grinned and said, "Trainees don't get tired. Do pushups."

All this time we had to juggle our heavy duffle bags, usually between our legs. The sergeants were not happy unless they could see dirt on our noses from doing pushups. For 10 weeks, anytime we were outside we had to run. If we were in line for chow, we ran in place. Before we entered the mess hall, we had a series of exercises to do, and if we messed up on one, we had to do it over. The last one was a horizontal ladder we had to "walk" using our hands, and if we missed a rung, we had to start over. With my light build, I was like an orangutan.

After basic, they put a lot of pressure on us to go airborne, which meant parachuting out of airplanes. At that time I was not afraid of heights, but that was too much. If I went to Vietnam, I did not want to be floating down as an easy target. Whoever said, "If at first you don't succeed, try again" did not know about sky diving. Strike one, and you're hamburger. I remembered my grandfather's advice: "Don't volunteer for anything." If I had a choice, I turned it down.

## Advanced Infantry Training

Then without leave, I was shipped to Ft. Jackson, SC, for another 10 weeks of Advanced Infantry Training (AIT). We had been there only a couple of days when we had our first assembly. There were several hundred of us in the auditorium.

The very first thing the company commander said was, "You're wondering if you're going to Vietnam. That's why you're here. All of you are going over so make the best of your training because the lives of your fellow soldiers and your own life will depend on how well you learn to defend yourself and others. Some of you won't make it back."

That was definitely motivation, but my heart sank again, and I was in a blue funk for days. I talked to one man who was about 10 years older than me, and he said:

"I've enlisted with one purpose in mind, to die. My life is miserable, I don't have the guts to kill myself, plus I don't want to embarrass my family. When I get to Vietnam, I'll volunteer for hazardous duty."

He did just that, and he died. He received a bronze star for bravery and a purple heart. I'm sure his family was proud and never knew his real motivation.

After AIT (Advanced Infantry Training), I had a month leave and then left for Vietnam. Ruth's mother gave me a going away party the night before I left, and I sat in a corner, not paying Ruth any attention. Two years later, Ruth would be my beloved wife (now 43 years), but marriage was not in my mind that night. I was so down that my countenance was what one grandfather called the mule face—long and sad. He used to say that when I was down, my face was so long that I could eat my dinner through a stove pipe. I was leaving the next day for Vietnam, and would I ever see anyone in this room again, my mother, my brother, Ruth (whom I barely knew), my grandmothers? The next day, as the jet pulled away from the dock in Memphis, I thought my heart would crush, I could not help but cry, and I wondered **what in the world the Lord was doing interrupting my life at its beginning**. It seemed like such a waste. I knew I was not immune to death. Thoughts tumbled after one another, gaining speed like a snow ball downhill. I was miserable.

# Chapter 5: In Vietnam

Once in Vietnam, we had about two weeks of in-country training to learn about insects, spiders, snakes, and especially booby-traps. Unfortunately, I could find all the booby traps—with my feet—which only confirmed the notion that I was going to die, alone, on the other side of the world from everyone I loved. Why was the Lord doing this to me? **Talk about bad timing**; it seemed that I had no time left on planet earth.

There were the dangers of the bamboo vipers whose bite usually resulted in death. Doesn't the Lord know that? And the rats were the size of cats, and they played in bunkers at night, squeaking and biting one another. We used to argue over who would get to stomp the rats when we tore down bunkers to move. Right after we moved in, the rats followed. We had as much success keeping them out as we did keeping out water. Bees were the size of hummingbirds, and you could hear their wings as they went by. A hornet came in my bunker one afternoon, and it was so large I could see the lines in its face. I went to sleep each night to the tune of a thousand voice soprano choir—mosquitoes. Did I mention that I hate mosquitoes?

But the wildlife was manageable compared to incoming artillery, such as 60 mm mortars that were more a nuisance than anything else, the 82 mm mortars they shot at us that were deadly (I was responsible for mortars also, 81 mm and then the 4.2 inch mortars; four deuce, we called them), and worst of all were the incoming 122 mm rockets. Our bunkers were protection enough against the mortars, but you just prayed your bunker was not hit by a rocket. It would be body bag time.

There were so many occasions I could have been killed, and other times I should have been killed, that I probably would not remember them all, but I kept a daily diary. I will mention only several of **God's timing miracles**.

On August 14th, 1967, we began Operation Benton (ended August 31), which was an offensive operation to go after the North Vietnamese Army, who were well trained and well supplied. I had been in Vietnam over a month, and except for the occasional sniper, had not seen any action. Sgt. Sledge was my squad leader. They told us to expect heavy casualties. My stomach was having those flip-flops again, and I was under a dark cloud. We were lined up in single file with all our gear, ready to go to the helipad to be airlifted to the battle when my squad leader came to me:

"Crenshaw, I was told to leave one man behind to resupply the choppers while we're in the field, and you're it."

"I'll be glad to stay behind, Sergeant."

My face instantly turned from a long mule face to happy monkey face in about one second. Several times a day I had to be at the helipad to load supplies on the helicopters; otherwise, I read in my tent and went to see movies at night. When my best friend in Vietnam (Salvatore Gallo, called Sal) returned, he said:

"Curt, it was bloody. We lost many of our guys, like 'Shane' who was shot in the legs before he could get out of the chopper. He'll probably go home, but he'll never be the same. Others will be going home in body bags."

**Once again, God's timing spared me at the last possible minute but right on time.** He was teaching me faith and patience, but I hate patience. I do not pray for patience, for that means trials (James 1:2-4).

## Mortar Competition

Gallo and I had been trained in the 81 mm mortars in AIT at Ft. Polk, LA, and Ft. Jackson, SC, respectively, May-June. Soldiers never knew if they would actually serve in the area of their training (called M.O.S., Military Occupational Specialty), but all had been trained to use the M-16. We might be put in the jungle to carry an M-16. It would be much better for Gallo and me to stay in mortars as then we would be carried by truck or chopper wherever we needed to go, avoiding most booby traps.

In October, the brigade commander decided to have competition between all the mortar squads in the 196th Light Infantry Brigade. There were many such squads, and we wondered why, in a war zone, would they play war? We had already been well trained so this seemed to be harassment. Nevertheless, we had no choice, and I was the gunner. I don't recall how many were in our squad, but I would guess about eight. To my astonishment, we won the whole competition. We were given an in-country R & R which I immediately took, knowing that things change and we might not get it later. Some ended up losing it when we got a "new king [captain] who did not know Joseph" (Exodus 1:8).

But what was the point to it all? The Lord of glory, who rules all, knew that most of the mortar squads would be made into M-16 rifle squads to go into the jungle. But since we had won the competition, we became the leading mortar squad in our battalion, and wherever headquarters went, we went—by truck or chopper—for the remainder of our time in Vietnam. **God's timing was at the last minute, but right on time.**

## Australia

In late March and early May of 1968, I had opportunity for R. & R. out of country so I took advantage of it. We had choices, such as Tokyo and Bangkok, which were the two most popular places. But there was only one reason to go to either of those places—prostitutes. I did not want to soil my reputation or be subject to that temptation so I chose Sydney, Australia. While on the charter plane to Sydney, a fellow soldier, whom I had never met, sat down beside me after we were in the air. He wanted us to team up to find prostitutes. I told him of my faith in Christ, and he made an excuse to leave, never returning to that seat. After we landed, a woman gave an hour presentation of what we could do, including how to find the "birds," which here we call "chicks." I could not believe it. Then she said, snickering, "If anyone is interested, Billy Graham is conducting a crusade." So that is where I went each night. But guess what else I looked up as soon as I was settled in Sydney. Right, bowling lanes. It was still in my blood.

# Chapter 6: Three Days of Death

The worst three days of my life (so far), and the most concentrated fighting I had in Vietnam, were May 10-12, 1968, full blown Tet Offensive. The Tet Offensive began on January 30, 1968 and ended sometime in August that same year. This Offensive was the time when the North Vietnamese Army (NVA) began their great push to rid South Vietnam of U.S.A. forces. The NVA were well trained and well supplied with weapons, unlike the "pajama bottoms" as we called those who shot at us from the rice paddies. It was well planned, and we lost a lot of men. One of the worst battles of the Tet Offensive was called Kham Duc, which also referred to an Army base next to the Laotian border in the middle of the jungle. You'll find numerous references to Kahm Duc on the internet.

For our purposes, all we need to know is that General William Westmoreland had decided to build-up the defenses of the Kham Duc Special Forces camp by sending in reinforcements, and I was part of that reinforcement. The camp had a large air strip, and the idea was that the US Army could conduct bombings from that secured site. I was part of the 196th Light Infantry Brigade, and our assigned weapons were primarily 81 mm mortars, which could be lobbed over hills into the enemy's back pocket.

We were flown in a C-130 from the city of Hue in the north to Kham Duc mid-afternoon May 10th, 1968, but unknown to us—or to the high command, I hope—the NVA had begun to surround this camp. We were flown in as reinforcements to the Green Beret, although they were usually our reinforcements. When we landed, we were ordered off the back of the plane in a hurry. As we ran for cover, there were mortars, 60 mm and 82 mm, dropping around us like hail stones. We were at an airstrip in the middle of nowhere, with nothing but very dense jungle all around us. It was not long after we ran off the C-130 that the incoming mortar rounds stopped pelting us. My diary says I weighed about 145 pounds, and that I had about 100 pounds of equipment.

The platoon sergeant who was over all the mortars was Sgt. Johnson, a lifer, as we called one who was a career soldier. He was a black man, about five feet ten inches, and extremely prejudiced against whites. He made our lives miserable when we were in a safe area. I had not endeared myself to him, for while on radio watch one night I discovered some porn, and I wrote on the back Matthew 5:28: "Whoever looks at a woman to lust for her has already committed adultery with her in his heart." It was against military law to have pornographic material, and I certainly did not know it belonged to Sgt. Johnson. But he knew who had written those words, so he sent for me. He began to ream me out for destroying private property, saying what he was going to do to me. Sal Gallo, our squad leader at that time, stepped in, and he blasted Johnson, saying that if he did one thing against me, he would tell the captain what the nature of that private property was and to whom it belonged. Johnson dropped the issue.

In the early morning of May 11th, Sal, had us set up our 81 mm mortar in a trench that was shaped like the letter "L", and our squad had one of the six mortars. The trench was about four feet deep, eight or so feet wide, and about 30 feet long in our part of the "L". We were on the end with two other guns between us and the bend in the "L". Sgt. Johnson told Gallo that he wanted us on an outpost. Sal, being Italian as well as one who looked out for his men, strongly objected and said we were already set up in the trench. Though Johnson could have ordered us to go on the outpost, he sent another squad.

Later that day, incoming mortar rounds began raining on us again, and that afternoon Sgt. Pigg, whose name I found on the Vietnam wall a few years ago, had his head blown off. He was in a narrow trench, stuck his head up with perfect timing to a mortar round that landed just outside the trench, and just that quick, he was gone. My friend Bennett with artillery was also killed shortly after Pigg; he had been such a nice guy. War is awful; you can talk to a person one second and the next second he is gone forever. I wondered how Sgt. Pigg's and Bennett's families back home would respond. I knew I could be next, but other things occupied my mind, like staying alive.

We did not eat all day, and had only eaten one meal the day before. Things calmed down for the rest of the day, and we continued to make our home in the trench with our 81 mm mortar. We stacked a pile of 81 mm rounds in one corner; must have been 50 or more of them. A lot of rounds could be used in a short period with heavy firing, even though only firing one at a time.

I found out later that on May 11th, once Westmoreland realized his mistake in ordering Kham Duc reinforced, reversed himself and ordered Kham Duc to be evacuated. However, we were already in process of being decimated. By late afternoon the next day (May 12), Kham Duc belonged to the NVA.

## All Dead

We tried to sleep in our trench the night of May 11th. It rained off and on all night. At 3:15 A.M., May 12, all hell broke loose. We were not facing the "pajama bottoms" but, being next to the Laotian border, we faced the NVA. We had four of our outposts surrounding our position. They hit all four simultaneously so we could not use our mortars to support all of them. We had to pick one. They also hit artillery at the same time to keep them from helping the outposts. Only one outpost made it back, and it lost one man. The men who made it back from the one outpost were running like dogs from a lion, and screaming. They were bloody, but not too badly injured. Recon (reconnaissance) was wiped out, about six men.

The outpost where my squad had almost been assigned the day before was hit with a human wave attack. The last one left was Lt. Ransbottom, whose last words over the radio are still ringing in my ears: "I just killed one in the doorway." Then silence. I also found his name on the Vietnam wall. **God's timing** had spared me being on that outpost when platoon Sgt. Johnson put another squad there because of Sal's objections; now they were all dead.

About 6:00 A.M. a Chinook came in with only the crew on board, but was hit as it was trying to land, and dropped like a rock from about 200 feet. It exploded and was reduced to just burning grass. It all seemed surreal, like I was watching a John Wayne war movie, except that I was in it, and people were actually dying around me.

The outpost I was supposed to be on was close to our position, and the NVA were on that hill firing directly at us. Since all our men there were dead, someone called in an airstrike on that position. I gasped at what I saw: there were three WWII prop planes, flying in formation, *slowly* circling to get position. Flying so slowly, they were easy targets. When they were positioned, one after the other they dive-bombed, dropping large rounds of napalm that made the hill light up like a city block at night. Napalm would burn into the skin and was virtually impossible to extinguish. When the third plane dove in to drop its load, the whole hill came alive with shooting, and the plane caught on fire. The pilot bailed out, but made an easy target floating down into the jungle. After a few seconds, he went limp. Why would they send slow prop planes instead of fast jets? We were being overcome. The NVA had silenced artillery, and they were pelting our six mortars in the "L" shaped trench.

Our whole outfit was desperate for backup, or none of us would make it out alive. Suddenly, about a quarter of a mile from our position (or less), the dirt began jumping into the air 100 feet, and more. Then a whole line of dirt was going up with many explosions, and we realized we had that backup—it was a B-52 airstrike, and in the exact places we knew the NVA were. The jets were too high for us to see or hear. Spontaneously, our squad stood up and began cheering, but then something told me to duck. As soon as I did, an 82 mm mortar landed just outside our trench, and it sprayed Jim McVay, Smith, Carl Jones, and my best friend, Sal Gallo. If I had not ducked, I would have taken the whole load as I was between them and the explosion. **Talk about split second timing!** One man had no flight jacket on but a helmet, and most of the shrapnel hit his helmet. Another man had no helmet on but a flight jacket, and most of his shrapnel went into his flight jacket, indeed, going through it. Both were spared death. I patched them up, and then took care of Gallo, who was injured in the arm and shoulder area rather severely. When the medics took the injured to a Red Cross chopper to safety and medical attention, only I and an atheist were left in my squad, whose name I shall call "Ray."

Sgt. Johnson, who had been so prejudiced against us, was now risking his life to save ours. He took several wounded from our squad across open territory to put them on choppers to see them to safety, getting hit several times with shrapnel. I heard that later he received the Silver Star, but never did know for sure. He came to our part of the trench and said to "Ray" and me: "Take down your gun, we're getting out of here." That was definitely good news!

"Ray" and I proceeded to disassemble our 81 mm gun. I leaned over to disengage the barrel from the base plate, when a mortar round, 82 mm I think, landed at my feet. I was holding the barrel across my chest, and "Ray" and I were blown backwards. The barrel was dented, but I was not touched, and considering that I was looking down on it, it does not seem mathematically possible. "Ray" was hit in the chest. You've heard the expression, "No atheist in a fox hole," but "Ray" was one. Yet when he thought he was going to die, he cried and wailed. Atheism may be passable to live by but not to die by.

I patched him with a cellophane bandage to make the entrance wound to his chest air tight so his lungs would not collapse. Once he got out of the hospital, he was his old self again, railing against God.

Thirty seconds after I had "Ray" patched up, another enemy round landed on the lip of the trench, just above the pile of 81 mm mortar rounds. If it had been over another two inches, I would have been vaporized. Now I don't mean to imply that His sovereign Majesty, the great King Jesus, is in the ambulance business, sending an angel at the last minute to guide the mortar so it would not hit the ammo pile. He may have done that, but it was **all** planned, not an ambulance sent to an almost foiled plan. He could have made me avoid these three days altogether, but through every detail I learned, in a way that I could never learn out of books, what it means to have a sovereign God to watch over me. "Ray" was taken by Johnson to a medical chopper. I was now the only one left from my squad.

Suddenly I heard loud shouting and bursts of automatic weapons about 70 yards away at the perimeter. The fighting was very intense, and I thought there was a human wave attack, which had happened the night before we got there, unknown to us until we had been at the location for 24 hours. The guns were blazing, increasing in intensity, and men were screaming. I leaned over the edge of the trench, pointed my M-16 in the direction of the deafening noise, expecting any second to see hundreds of NVA burst through the thickets. I prayed silently: "Well, Lord, this is it. Here I come." I was determined not to be taken alive and was going to force them to shoot me. As quickly as it began, it all stopped. I never knew what happened, but once again **God's timing was scary, but there**.

Sgt. Johnson told me to forget the mortar, to get to the airstrip and get on the third Chinook. That was good news. The airstrip was about 75 yards from where I was, and that meant going across mostly open territory. That was bad news. He ordered me to leave everything behind except my M-16, which never left our sides, not even when we ate, slept, or took the occasional shower (about every two weeks). But I never fired it at the enemy, though I killed some with the mortar. When the firing slowed down, I took off for the airstrip. The firing got heavy again, and I found shelter in the midst of a pile of twisted steel that had once been some kind of equipment. As I sat there I thought:

> "I'm on the other side of the world. All my friends have been flown to safety. I hope none have died. I'm the only one left in my squad, and all my worldly possessions are in a water proof bag I cannot take with me. All I have is You, O Lord, and well, that is enough."

When firing let up again, I ran to the airstrip. I was disgusted that I could not take anything with me, so I did one of the dumbest things in my life—I went back and got mine and Gallo's bags, across 75 yards of open territory each way, and then returned to the airstrip. Sgt. Johnson must not have known that, or I would have been in serious trouble.

I watched three Chinooks circling some distance away, and I had been directed to get on the third one. The first one came in, landed quickly with a thump, hurriedly loaded up with men, took off slowly to gain altitude, and was shot down, though it did not fall and explode but the blades kept turning so that it made a very bumpy landing. Most of the men would live, for the moment. But unknown to all, a human wave attack was being formed and would kill all the survivors. The second Chinook repeated the same scenario.

The third one bounced on the asphalt of the air strip, and men scrambled to get on it. The precedent was not good! I lingered, lying on the ground, wondering what to do. If I stayed, I would face all the incoming rounds and possible death, and maybe a human wave attack. If I got on it, I might be shot down; so far 100% had been. As I pondered, a mortar round landed about five feet from my head, only one piece went into my right forearm, and I'm right handed. I recall being surprised that it did not hurt. Another man was hit from the same round, but he was standing up and hurt badly and began screaming. His buddy took care of him, and I never knew if he lived. The shrapnel in my forearm and the other soldier screaming made my feet get on the Chinook, one of the last three on it, and my captain the last one. The captain got on the intercom system at the rear and commanded the pilot not to go over the area where the other two had been shot down, but apparently he had no choice. Everyone was totally silent, listening for the anti-aircraft guns to sound, but we never heard them, and I think I may know why.

About that same time, three jets were flying in very fast, coming up a very wide but dry river bed, firing 20 mm cannons. They were angels of mercy for us, but if they did not save us, I don't know what did. According to my diary, the last men left at the airstrip called in a B-52 airstrike on themselves as there was no more hope. I only read about that later in the military news, and still have the clipping, and my heart just sank. "Why war, O Lord God, why something so terrible when men kill one another on sight without even knowing one another?" Of course, part of the answer is that it demonstrates how horribly sinful we are. I would read in the military newspaper a few days later:

> 9 Aircraft Lost As Allies Give Up Surrounded Post
> (16 May 1968 [date of the article])

> Allied forces abandoned the U.S. Special Forces
> camp at Kham Duc to the North Vietnamese at a heavy
> cost in lives and equipment.

After the Chinook had flown a couple of minutes, I knew we were safe. I watched a man on the floor of the Chinook die, and I bowed my head in thanksgiving that I was spared. **Once again, the Lord God had delivered me, at the very last minute, but right on time**.

## Hospital

I was flown to LZ Ross (Landing Zone Ross) from the battle field, my wound looked at, then classified as not serious, but nevertheless flown to Da Nang hospital where I was treated. I was ambulatory, so I walked into the surgical building, a half-moon shaped metal structure, with men undergoing "minor" surgery as I walked a long aisle between two rows of sufferers lying on beds, all the way to the end of the building. Seeing men groan as young interns dug for metal was not my idea of mental health. Just as my intern was about to deaden my forearm, there were incoming rockets with their distinctive crackling sound. In the last three days, I had eaten once, slept only a few hours, and what nerves I had remaining had unraveled to a single thread. I was put under the bed, given a flight jacket (not exactly bullet "proof" but at least resistant), all lights turned off, and remained there, shivering on the concrete like a wet dog, for about two hours. Finally, the lights came back on and the young intern returned, tried to deaden my arm, but apparently did not know what he was doing, as when he began to dig, I had excruciating pain. While holding my hand in one position, the rest of me flopped around on the table like a fish out of water. After what seemed like an hour, but was probably five minutes, he said he would do more harm getting it out than leaving it. I spent the rest of the night shivering on the concrete floor with my flight jacket, teeth clicking like a typewriter.

The next morning I was flown to Cam Rahn Bay hospital. There an experienced surgeon agreed to leave the shrapnel in. It would be nine years later, at the VA hospital in Memphis, where the shrapnel would be removed when it began to give me trouble. (That is another story. Many times I was bumped from the surgery schedule for more serious patients when the surgeon in charge finally told me to shut up, that I would be taken to surgery with an emergency appendectomy! I made sure I was awake in surgery when I heard them say, "Here comes our emergency appendectomy that involves taking the growth from the right forearm!" You have to love them!)

While I was lying in the hospital in Vietnam, a high ranking officer came and gave me a hearty handshake, and without thinking I grabbed his hand with mine when he surprised me by extending his, which caused shooting pain. He gave me a Purple Heart. Later, I would also receive the Bronze Star for valor, for helping to save the lives of the men in my squad. I expected the Purple Heart, which is rewarded for being injured in action, but the Bronze Star was a complete surprise. I still have both.

I did not know Gallo's status, if he survived, where he was, if he were sent home, but then suddenly on May 26th, 9:45 P.M., he showed up at our outfit again. We hugged and talked for hours, and we would both go home around the middle of July. We were best friends in Vietnam, and watched each other's back. He had immigrated to the USA from Italy when he was twelve, and learned English by speaking it. Thus, he had two first languages, Italian and English. As the Navy SEALs would say, we were brothers without the same mother. One can develop deep friendships quickly when you know you may have to die for another. But at a more basic level, we were (are) brothers in Christ, having the same heavenly Father by faith in the Son of God.

## Other Close Calls

I have not told all the close calls I had in Vietnam, that would probably take another book. There was not only the enemy, but as the comic character Pogo once said, "I have seen the enemy, and they is us." There were constant accidents, such as men *playing* with hand grenades, which sent some home in body bags. Or, not paying attention to the rules about charges that went on our 4.2 inch mortar rounds, which sent more home in body bags or permanently disabled others, and I had just walked away seconds before. There were the ever present booby traps, snipers, not to mention snakes (though I never saw one but others did), and other pests, and so on. The time a hand grenade was dropped at chow, and I had just walked out of the screened-in hut. The time Gallo saved me from a major booby trap. The time the ammo dump caught on fire, and I ran down the hill naked. I could continue, but my point has been made.

## Lessons Learned

What did I learn from two years in the Army? If you recall, I was very undisciplined in my work, and my grades suffered, both in engineering and at the Bible college. Then I had an idol in my life, bowling. Moreover, I was pursuing the wrong vocation, which was engineering, but should have been the ministry.

So what is the point? Out of dozens of times I just missed getting injured very seriously, or killed, I came back with only one hit: my right forearm. What did that do to my bowling? It permanently removed it. I could bowl for a few games, but then I would suffer with throbbing. There was now no way I could make bowling my career.

Moreover, those two years completely changed my attitude toward life. My lazy and undisciplined life became disciplined, and I still love studying. My grades improved significantly. I studied seven consecutive years, three years in Bible college and then four years in seminary. Some get burned out with studying, but I never have. The Lord worked in my heart a change that has lasted all these decades. When I got out of the Army, I had only two things on my brain: Ruth and Bible college. That was all that mattered. On July 25th, 1969, I married the greatest woman I could have, a gift straight from God, prepared just for me her whole life, and I prepared for her. We have never questioned our marriage, and we vowed never to use the "D" word, "divorce." (We recognize that some divorces are legitimate.) We have kept that vow. She helped to put me through Bible college and seminary, and has encouraged me and our ministry all these years. She teaches ladies Bible studies and conducts conferences at churches. It took two years, but the Lord Jesus took away the bowling, changed my attitude toward life, and gave me a wonderful wife. The Lord had known what He was doing when that letter said "Greeting," and had required that I trust Him. I wanted to live by sight, but He had not allowed that. He was in charge, not me. **His timing had been perfect**.

# Chapter 7: Bible College and Seminary

When we married, Ruth was working for a plastic florist, and the boss was terrible about interrupting our lives by calling her in to work on the spur of the moment. One Sunday afternoon we were taking a nap when her boss called.

"Hello."

"This is Mr. 'Smith.' Is Ruth there?"

I said, "Mr. 'Smith,' per our agreement when we married, Ruth would like to have Sundays off."

"Well, ok, but I really need her today."

"Sorry, but we're honoring our agreement."

Ruth asked, "Who was that?"

I responded in disgust: "Who do you think? You're going to have to get another job, as he will not leave you alone."

After that phone call, Ruth began to look for another job, and found a good one at Leader Federal Savings and Loan, which she had for the three years I attended the Bible college.

The Bible college did not allow newlyweds to attend until a year after marriage, but our marriage was the impetus to change the policy of the college so I entered as a full time student the month after our marriage. **God's timing was at it again**. I had failed three courses that I had to take over (I received the academic award at graduation), and I was able to transfer some credits from the engineering college so I graduated in three years (May 1972) with a B.A., the first one in our extended family as far as anyone knew.

Then another problem arose as I approached graduation. When I entered the Bible college, it was not accredited, but the seminary I wanted to attend was accredited. One cannot be accepted by an accredited school from a non-accredited one, at least to get a degree, but only a few months before I graduated from the college, it became accredited. I was the first student to attend Dallas Theological Seminary from Mid-South Bible College with an accredited degree. I entered seminary in September 1972. **God's timing, once again, was at the last minute, but right on time.**

## Two Jobs Quickly Given

We went to Dallas in early June of 1972 to find a place to live and to see if Ruth could find another bank job. She got a job at Dallas Federal Savings and Loan in 24 hours. (**Talk about timing!**) Her experience at the Savings and Loan in Memphis was a good reference. I had not needed to work in Bible college, but I would in seminary.

After we moved to Dallas in late July, Ruth discovered that there was a minimum wage job that a teacher was heading up for the summer at the Savings and Loan. She had teens working under her, but I might work there until something else opened. I was 27. The Savings and Loan was beginning a microfilm department to film all the old records back to the early 1900s. It was tedious, mindless work, as we were alphabetizing millions of records to film. I was told by Mr. Robert Bourne, the main boss, to work until 4:30 P.M., which I did. However, my immediate boss was leaving early and so were the teens. The time cards were not on a machine, but each person was on his honor to sign in and out accurately.

One day after all were gone except me, Mr. Bourne came in around 4:15. He said,

"Where is everyone?"

I said, "They left."

He looked at the time cards, and discovered that they had signed out at 4:30, including my immediate boss. Mr. Bourne was livid. He fired her, and made me the new head of the microfilm department.

I said anxiously, "I know nothing about microfilming."

He responded, "Neither do we. You'll be trained on the machine when we purchase it. What do you say?"

"The teens will be returning to school when summer ends, and if you let me hire seminary students, no one will have to look over their shoulders; we can do more work with less employees."

He agreed.

I suggested using the phone book as our model for alphabetizing, and he thought that was great. It worked well. Guess how long it took to complete filming the records? Seminary was four years, beginning in September 1972 and ending in May 1976. The job at the Savings and Loan began in July 1972 and ended in May 1976. The month of graduation we finished filming all the records, and our jobs ended. **Talk about timing!** This provided jobs for me and several other seminarians for our seminary career, and we were paid substantially more than minimum wage. Mr. Bourne and I got along fabulously for those four years. He was Christian Science, and though I talked to him several times about the Lord, he did not convert. Yet God used him, much as He had used Cyrus, to accomplish His purpose.

## First House

After a few months into seminary, we found a house to move into, and borrowed $4,400 from Shussie, my grandmother, and we got a twenty year loan on the remaining $16,000. The house was in a nice residential area of Dallas, three bedrooms, large living room, small den, two-car carport, and fenced in back yard with a gold fish pond complete with large gold fish! Our monthly note was less than we had been paying for a two bedroom apartment, $116.68. (I'm sure of that figure.) The day we moved in was April 1st, 1973, April Fool's Day, and we had been fooled. It was raining hard, both outside and inside. The couple we bought the house from had lied to us about the condition of the house, failing to disclose that the tar and gravel roof leaked terribly. A fellow seminary student showed me how to put on shingles, and for months, every spare moment was spent raking off the rocks and putting on a new shingled roof. It never leaked again.

Ruth and I had never had two nickels to rub together, but our theme verse from the time we began dating was Matthew 6:33:

> "Seek ye first the kingdom of God and His righteousness, and all these things will be added to you."

The "things" in context are material, such as food and clothing. We believed in working, but we trusted in the Lord for the details. (Now at ages 67 and 66, without a lot of money to retire, we still trust Him.) But we lived hand to mouth in seminary days. Our finances got worse, for after two years in seminary, we had our first child, Ruth cut back to part-time work, and I had to work more, the GI Bill had been used up, and my half-brother came to live with us.

One day as we came home from work and school, I said:

"What's for supper?"

Ruth quipped: "We don't have anything."

"How much money do you have?" I asked. "I don't have any."

She said, "I have about fifty cents."

As I checked the mail at home, I turned to her: "There is a check here for $10." In 1974, ten dollars would buy a decent amount of food.

A few days later, I found in my campus mail box (which was 666!), a white envelope. I turned to a friend: "Can you believe that? Here is a plain white envelop with three $20 dollar bills in it."

When that was spent, one professor, Dr. Evans, called Ruth at home, where she was tending our newborn son.

"This is Dr. Evans at the seminary, and I don't mean to pry, but I hear that you're having financial difficulties. If you don't mind, can you tell about how much you owe presently."

"We just figured the bills, and we owe $150."

"Ok, thank you."

A few minutes later the door bell rang. "Hello, I'm Dr. Evans, and here is a check for $150. Consider it a gift from the Lord." I never had Dr. Evans for a class, and I never knew how he heard that we were having financial difficulties.

Ruth's brother and sister-in-law, Jim and Teresa Hanks, supported us with their monthly giving, as did my mother and one grandmother who was able to do so. (The other grandmother did not have the money.) And so it went for four years, and we kept a diary, which I've lost. **God's financial faithfulness was incredible, day by day, timing always at the last minute, but always on time**, just as He promised in Matthew 6:33.

## Career Choice?

It was time to graduate. A friend asked me: "Now that you're finishing seminary, what are you going to do?"

"I don't know, but I can tell you three things I'm not going to do: pastor a church, move back to Memphis, and teach in the Bible college where I graduated."

So now what was I to do after graduation? I was too scared to take a church. I found an ad in a Christian book catalog announcing for Hebrew scholars to translate the first Hebrew Interlinear ever done. My major in seminary was both Greek and Hebrew. I applied and got the job, which was only for the summer of 1976. Thus, Ruth and I rented our Dallas home to friends, who needed it only for the summer (**perfect timing!**), and we drove to Wilmington, DE. There I spent eight to ten hours a day, along with other men, translating the Hebrew Old Testament into literal English. It was a fun job. Ruth and our two-year old son, Treis (pronounced Trace), struggled to live in a motel suite of sorts.

On the way to Wilmington from Dallas, we stopped in Memphis to see our friends and relatives, and I met a pastor of a church just outside Memphis, in Munford. We quickly became friends.

After the Hebrew project was over, it was time to drive back to Dallas, but Ruth and I had no jobs and no money. We stopped again in Memphis, and I looked up my new friend, Tom, the pastor in Munford, and he said he was going to leave the church, and he wondered if I wanted to candidate for it. That was the **only** open door. I was well received and got the pastorate, so we went back to Dallas to sell our house and move to Munford, TN. **At the very last minute, but on time, the Lord Jesus had come through again.** After my "prophecy" of the three things I would not do, guess who was sovereign? In six months, I was doing all three: I had moved back to the Memphis area, was pastor of a church, and the Bible college asked me to teach part time. Good grief, does God have a sense of humor?

# Chapter 8: School Problems

Ruth, it appears that our theology is changing so maybe, if something else opens, we should take a year or two off from the pastorate until we get things settled."

"Perhaps you're right, sweet heart."

Very shortly after that conversation a good friend, David Werner, was made headmaster of a Christian school and needed a Bible teacher. After my first two weeks at Labelle Haven Baptist Christian School with junior high students, it seemed I only had three choices: resign, burn down the school, or suicide! I chose perseverance instead.

The school year turned out to be one of the most profitable ministries I've ever had, with several conversions amidst a tragedy that led to a campus revival, an outpouring of God's Spirit. There were two ninth grade boys who were best friends, and they liked to go hunting together. "Paul" was spending the night with Newt, they planned to go hunting that coming weekend, and they were looking at Newt's new shotgun. The phone rang, and unknown to "Paul," Newt had put a round in the shotgun. Newt answered the phone, handing the gun to "Paul," who subsequently pulled the trigger. The whole load went into Newt's head. He died instantly.

I did not have a home room as I was hired not only to teach Bible but also to develop a Bible curriculum, primarily for the upper level (sixth through the ninth grade). However, the morning after the tragedy, I took the home room of the ninth grade class. It was a very difficult time because it was a small school, and all the students were very close friends. The headmaster closed the school for the rest of the week, and everyone went to the funeral. Here is what I wrote for the school annual:

Newt Jenkins: Remembering and Anticipating

A person could not help liking Newt. He was easy going, not hard to get along with, always in a good humor, and never met an enemy. Newt was like a melody in a song; he was often the basis for harmony to those around him. But Newt's "song" was stopped short on February 9, 1978. At first, perhaps, we asked the question "Why?" Why did God take one so young—only fourteen years old—and so new to life? Yet we knew that the infallible God never errs. Instead of being bitter toward our Lord for the time we did not have Newt, we thanked the all wise and sovereign God for the time we did enjoy him. But the note does not end on a sad refrain for the Lord God omnipotent arranges all the music. Newt's home-going was sooner than ours. He was a true believer in the Lord Jesus Christ. . . . absent from the body is to be at home with the Lord (2 Cor. 5:8). . . . (and about another half page)

The school did not continue due to lack of funds, but I received many kind letters of recommendation from the principal and parents, which I took to the next school where I taught, Spurgeon Academy.

We had a mini-revival on campus there also when a student in my senior church history class asked about the Gospel. I began teaching him Romans at lunch. It was not long that other students joined us, and we eventually had about 20 each day, going through Romans verse by verse. Again, that school also closed at the end of the year for lack of funds. With that track record, someone suggested that I hire myself out to the IRS!

By this time (1979) I had two children but no job. I found a part-time job with a very gracious man who owed a pool cue plant, Bob Meucci. He paid well, so I was working for him. Also, I was helping to start a Presbyterian church (PCA), but at the time there was no money to pay me.

Suddenly, an opportunity opened for me to teach Bible in a well established Christian high school. I could get free tuition for my kids, and I was unalterably committed to keep them out of the public schools (and managed to do so). Ruth and I always paid two things and in this order: tithe and tuition. I spoke to the head of the Bible department, took him a thick folder of the recommendations from my two previous school teaching jobs, my Th.M., and he was in pro-cess of setting up an interview for me with the head master. He thought I would be hired on the spot. It was exactly where I had been trained and where my heart was—Christian education.

I had told a fellow elder at the Presbyterian church, whom I shall call "Jake," of my upcoming interview, to please keep it confidential, that I just coveted his prayers. A few days later, "Jake" called me to say he had had an interview with the head master for that job, even though he already had a good job, making a lot more than the school paid. He had violated my confidence in him, all the time knowing how much I needed a job. The Bible department head was not aware of his interview, it seems. Several days later, "Jake" called again to say he had been offered and accepted the teaching job. I was floored. How could a brother in Christ do that to me? "Jake" was known as one who could start an argument with a thorn bush, and true to form, he was confrontational at the school and was soon let go.

My ego was crushed, for I had the equivalent of an earned doctorate but could not support my family. Once I graduated from high school, I had had three years of electrical engineering, three years of Bible college, four years of seminary, and one year in the graduate program for philosophy at the local university. Moreover, I had two years of teaching in Christian day schools with many letters of recommendation, and "Jake" had none of these, not even a college degree. What in the world was the Lord doing? Did God give me gifts only to taunt me in the use of them? I lost confidence in myself. Then I had a thought: the great Shepherd of the sheep was teaching me—through no deliverance—that He wanted **me**. He could use my talents anytime; it was **me** He loved. He wanted to change **me**, then He could use my talents better. I needed to get over my ego, and humbly serve Him where I was. If I wanted to be used in a larger way, I had to be faithful in a smaller way.

What made it more pungent is that the man apologized, sort of, so we continued together in the same church for about two more years. As he described his Bible classes when we were around one another at church functions, it was a constant reminder of what he had done and of my inability, or so it seemed at the time.

**So what was God's timing in this matter?** It was a lesson in perseverance, humility, and learning about human nature. It was excruciating not to be able to support my wife and children. I was down on myself and thought I was unfit for the ministry or for teaching. Yet God was teaching me to trust Him, not my efforts, not my self-reliance. But where was His timing?

# Chapter 9: Christian Book Store

As I was agonizing over what I would do now without a job, a friend came to town to look over the possibility of putting a Christian bookstore in Memphis. He had a number of them around the country. I invited him to stay at my townhouse, and after returning home he wrote me a letter to see if I knew of anyone who would want to manage the store, someone who knew Christian literature. That opportunity had my name on it. Plus, it was the **only** open door. Thus I spent the entire summer of 1979 in Los Angeles, CA, learning to manage a Christian book store. **Talk about timing!**

The store opened in Memphis in the fall of 1979. I did not like the location, but the hierarchy had not asked me for advice, at least until after the fact, even though I was lifelong Memphian. It was at Summer Ave. and the expressway loop. The pay was not great, $450 twice a month, but the store ministry was good, and I enjoyed meeting people and helping pastors choose good literature. I could sell books few could because of my Greek and Hebrew skills, and even taught the biblical languages at the store.

In the summer of 1980, we had terrible flooding in Memphis, the worst I know of to date, and it washed out several bridges, including the one where the store was. (I missed the collapse of one bridge by about a minute!) Even though the store was still accessible, it was difficult to get to the store, and as a result we lost sales.

To my utter shock, one day in the fall of 1980, my immediate boss, who had flown down unannounced from the main office in Grand Rapids, walked into the store to fire me for lack of sales, even though we were making bills. The bridge out did not make any difference to him. I would be allowed to stay while I found another job, but needed to look diligently. My assistant, Randy Middleton—and cousin, many times removed, we discovered years later—was also fired and was given about two weeks notice. The customer base strongly objected, and the big boss of the corporation called me to offer the job back, but I did not want to live under a guillotine, so I just asked to be allowed to stay long enough to find another job. **The timing here seemed to be terrible**, for I could not figure out why God wanted me out of the book store.

That Christmas of 1980 we had few presents for our two children, who never knew of our financial woes, and who loved what they received.

# Chapter 10: Fraud Scheme & Three Other Matters

A man I had come to know toward the end of my book store days, "Hugh," offered me a job selling insurance and investments. I couldn't sell ice to desert people at half price, but it seemed like a good opportunity while the church I was helping to start grew, to the point I could be supported.

Before I went to work at the firm, I called several older Christian business men in the Memphis area who knew of the company, and they all said it was 115 years old with a sterling reputation.

Thus, in early 1981, I left the book store to work for this company. (I was 36.) I recruited others, being promised overrides from their sales, and we all went to work for "Hugh," who in turn was a boss in the company. He appeared to be a Christian though shallow in his faith. He could pray and lead a Bible study with tears. It was nice to be able to offer people life insurance at a fraction of what they were paying and with often many times the coverage. It was so good that some were skeptical.

"Nothing could be that good," one client stated to me, "surely my life insurance company would not take advantage of me that badly."

He was wrong; they had, but I could not convince him so he kept his old life insurance policy, and I lost the sale. Yet I made other sales, and was at least supporting my family. On one occasion, "Hugh" paid me $1,000 in hundred bills in the presence of the men I had recruited, which was the first clue that something was wrong. He was trying to manipulate.

There was another thing that we were pushed to sell, an investment they called "investment grade diamonds." One disadvantage growing up in a sheltered Christian environment was that I was very naïve. I trusted people implicitly. But something did not seem right. Also, my paternal grandmother and wife did not trust "Hugh," but I had not learned to listen to women's intuition—big mistake! I had never heard of such an investment so I began to investigate. The diamonds were allegedly of high quality, allegedly graded by reputable and certified graders recognized throughout the world, who would put the diamond in a vacuum sealed plastic package with the grading on it. If the seal were broken, the grading was voided. I was really interested in selling insurance, but in time I became hooked on the investment. The money was good and the future potential seemed very good in these stones. They were said to appreciate about 20 to 40 percent a year, and controlled by De Beers to make sure they did, but I did not like the idea of a monopoly. I even got my good friend Richard involved in it, and we became greedy, or at least I did. We started a club that would purchase diamonds as a group. It never occurred to me that the diamonds were vastly overpriced.

The insurance sales were not going well, and all the pressure was to sell the stones. Something was wrong, but I could not figure out what. (In times like these, it is my custom to keep a diary.) I wanted to leave the job, but I had no place to go. I wrote, "Rats, God, why can't I run like Jonah. I can't even find a whale." I knew that when all doors were closed, I had no option but to face the current situation.

## Discovery

In June, I had a conversation with Allen Avin, a diamond dealer, whom I had just "happened" to stumbled across. (**God's timing strikes again.**) He kept his occupation a mystery as he often carried several hundred thousand dollars of diamonds to sell to jewelry stores. I met him where I had preached many times as a guest preacher in his Presbyterian church where he was an elder. Allen told me that the company I was working for was selling diamonds at a very high price. He was a wholesaler for Miller and Veit out of New York, NY. I told Richard immediately the bad news. Allen told Richard and me that he could sell us diamonds at half or less than my company was selling them, so naïve as we were, we went to my company to tell them they could save money! We did not know that they knew it, and were probably buying them for even less than half price. They were selling the stones vastly overpriced, pocketing the difference, and promising to buy them back at an appreciated price, but actually had no intention to repurchase them. The artificial price was a scam. As I was trying to sort this out, I suspected that it was also a pyramid scheme.

Then one night I recalled a conversation I had had with a friend who had mentioned that "Hugh," who had hired me, had had some legal problems in Mississippi. It was just a passing conversation that had not stuck in my mind at the time. I called him to find out if I had remembered correctly, and he gave me a couple of names. By the end of the night, I had talked to a half dozen people and found out that "Hugh" had spent a year in jail for selling stock in a radio station that did not exist. His method was to stay in a town long enough to make sales in his new adventure.

Where did he get the victims? He would walk the aisle at a moderate size Southern Baptist church where he could join on the spot. Then he would win the people's confidence with his winsome personality, give large sums of cash to the church, making sure someone knew it, and then sell them his latest scheme. He knew Christians were trusting and that they rarely pursued justice in the courts. He was making tens of thousands of dollars, and every check he got from someone, no matter how large, he would cash it. He left no bank trails.

Once I had an insurance policy that I had sold. It had required several signatures by the buyer, but I had forgotten to get it signed at one place. "Hugh" practiced the signature, and then signed it perfectly. He laughed and said, "I once got six months for that." We all laughed; it turned out to be true.

Then Richard and I took a graded stone to Allen at his office. He said he was the first official grader in the South.

Allen warned: "If you break the seal, the grading is no good, but that is the only way for me to grade it."

Since he was an elder in a reputable Presbyterian church, we trusted him, and our trust was not misplaced. We had to know if the stones were diamonds or zirconium. We broke the seal.

Allen advised us: "I do not want to see the grading, but I shall grade it independently."

So we waited a long 30 minutes or better, and finally he said, "It is a diamond, not zirconium, and I grade it as 0.54 carat, color E V V S1." That was exactly what our grading said. We breathed a sigh of relief, but now we had to get people's money back. I agonizingly told everyone to whom I had sold diamonds that they were vastly over priced, and that the company never had any intention of repurchasing them.

We discovered that the scheme went back to NY City to a man named "John." He was buying real diamonds, having them graded, but then selling them vastly over priced, promising quarterly appreciation, and to buy them back at the appreciated price whenever someone wanted to sell. The prices were not market prices, as they had said, and there was no appreciation, just pocketing the money. Once we began to blow the whistle and to demand our money back for our customers, things got ugly very quickly. I've wondered if we were dealing with the organized crime in NY, and still don't know for sure. "John" flew down from NY just to meet with Richard and me privately in a hotel room, and like sheep, we went, though we made sure others knew where we were. Here is the way the conversation went.

"John" said, "What seems to be the problem?"

Richard, "Well, obviously these diamonds are being sold at very high prices with promise to buy them back, but so far no one will do that. It appears that you are the ultimate source for these stones. We have a moral obligation to be honest with our clients so we want to sell the stones back, at least at the price they paid for them."

Of course, he quickly recognized how naïve we were, and he promised to buy back the stones, over time, for he wanted the scheme to continue. We managed to get some stones sold, but not all.

I got really angry and wanted to shut down the scheme. I went to "Hugh's" pastor with two others to tell him what "Hugh" was doing to the people in his congregation. I had documents and names and phone numbers and the testimony of the three of us that could verify my claims. He would not touch it, but said we need to "love" one another.

I angrily said, "Love is not allowing your sheep to be fleeced. What will the people say when they find out they have been sheared by 'Hugh,' and you could have stopped it." We left in disgust.

I went to the local attorney general, who said "things like this were very difficult to prove," which meant "go away." I visited the Securities and Exchange, but to no avail. I took my documents to the FBI since it was interstate, but they were very busy, and a month later an agent called me. Nothing was done. I was so frustrated to see people being defrauded while I watched.

## Bolt of Lightning

Then suddenly I recalled that I had a friend who was an investigator for one of the local TV news stations. I took him my story and the documents, and we went to one of the news casters. At first, he had trouble believing it. Then he said they might interview me for a blurb. As he and others at the station got into it and saw the magnitude, they did a five part series, Monday through Friday, six o'clock news, interviewing me. Law suits spewed out like lava, and that stopped the scheme.

Minutes before my story was first aired on Monday night, I called "Hugh's" pastor at home.

"Hello, is this Rev. 'Luvvy'?"

"Yes, it is."

"I'm Curtis Crenshaw, and I and two other men visited you about 'Hugh' defrauding your congregation with a bogus investment. You refused to do anything about it."

Clearing his throat.

"I thought you would want to know that I'm about to be on the 6:00 p.m. news , blowing the whistle, not only tonight, but for the other four nights this week as well, same time. I have named you as a silent accomplice who could have done something, but refused."

Long silence. He was utterly speechless. Not long after that, he left the church and moved out of state.

"Hugh" could not be sued since he had no visible assets, and he left town, going to Muscogee, OK where he was later put on trial for selling stock in a non-existent TV station. He took the stand, and with his smooth personality talked his way out of it. Then he was not making money fast enough so he changed his method: this time he robbed a bank at gun point, had some singing Dixie with their hands leaning on the walls, while others filled his bags! He wore motorcycle gloves and a dark helmet that no one could see what race he was. He left with about $50k. His wife, who may have been in on his schemes, most likely turned him in, as bank robbery was too much. Civil money schemes were one thing, but criminal bank robbery at gunpoint another. His cousin told me in 1992 that he was serving 15 years.

## No Job Again

I had stopped the scam, but I had no job again, a wife and two small children, no money, and in the midst of all that a church had turned me down as pastor for a non-biblical reason. I had worked with the church for six months, been their interim pastor, and they gave me every reason to think they were going to call me. The disappointment was painful, not only personally but financially. I had done the right thing to expose the fraud, but then it seemed my reward was no job. In late 1981, I became interim the pastor of a small congregation in Atoka, TN, about 20 miles north of Memphis, and was with them for five wonderful years. It was a very positive ministry, but was only part time.

Meanwhile, it was mid-1981, my jaw was dragging, and I was at one of the lowest points of my life. If it had not been for Richard, who hired me to mind his carpet store on Saturdays, and paid me a commission for any sales I made, I would not have made it.

I managed to get an afternoon paper route that my ever faithful wife took over. It was a driving route of about 80 miles. My son helped, and he was only seven. What an incredible family I had (have)! I approached Richard about putting out brochures in neighborhoods for his carpet company, and he said he had tried it with little success.

I said, "I don't have anything to lose so if you'll print them, I would like to try the areas outside the loop that you did not try." At age 36, with two degrees, one a four-year graduate degree, I was without job and at the bottom, hired by my best friend, who only had a high school diploma.

## Suicide, Not An Option

There were times I did not care if I lived or died, but I never thought to take my own life. Anyone can die; it takes courage to live, or better, it takes faith. My faith at times was weak, at other times it was stronger, and the whole year was like a roller coaster ride with loose rails. One thing I knew for sure was that God loved me, for He gave me His only Son to die for my sins and to raise Himself from the dead. I rested on that rock of truth, but wondered what my life was about. **God seemed far away, and His timing did not seem to be in tune with my needs.**

## Church Trial

While the fraud scheme, the church that rejected me, and an excruciating unmentioned trial (relative outside the home trying to commit suicide) were all going on, another Presbyterian church I was helping to form had a very recalcitrant elder, who was the same one who violated my confidence and took my job, "Jake." He was tearing up our church, leading a number of young, immature men in a wrong direction. We could not stop him, and his rebellion was spilling over into other Presbyterian churches in the city. No amount of talking did any good.

The Presbyterian way is confrontational, so we drew up charges, and indicted him. We had a church trial, and I was appointed the prosecutor. One cannot imagine the angst this causes everyone in the church, and we spent hours, and weeks, taking depositions and trying to get things worked out to avoid a trial. But "Jake" would hear none of it. The trial began. We called in other ministers from around the city where he had "disturbed the peace and purity of the church," as the technical language said, and they testified against him. After a few days of the trial, and when "Jake" saw that he would not prevail, he made a half-hearted apology, resigned as elder, and moved out of state. But the whole thing took months and left me drained.

## Autopilot

For much of 1981, with four ongoing, very intense trials—the fraud scheme, the church that turned me down, the unmentioned trial, and the church trial at another church—I was on autopilot. My wife had an 80 mile paper route, and I was putting out brochures. Much of the time I was numb. Intellectually, I knew the triumvirate: (1) use whatever human means I could to make things happen, for faith without works is dead (James 2:26), which included a lot of prayer; (2) obey Holy Scripture; (3) and trust God's providence. For example, God would not necessarily provide for me now in the same way He did while I was in seminary. The latter point was getting increasingly difficult. One other thing is important to mention. I would not use past providence to predict future providence. The future is God's domain, not mine. There were times I wanted to reword scripture. Instead of the "*love* of money" being the root of all evil, I wanted it to say the "*lack* of money" was (1 Tim. 6:10), and instead of "faith without *works* is dead" it seemed that "faith without *cash* was dead" (James 2:26).

Some say we should look at the cup of our lives as half full, not half empty. To me, that is a useless psychological gimmick that one uses to lift himself while standing on his hands. Such self-made people end up worshipping their creator—themselves. Rather, we must be like Jesus who *drank* the cup, for only then is grace applied just as Paul the Apostle accepted his thorn in the flesh and then received grace to bear it (2 Cor. 12:7-10). Grace is given at the point of need, not at the point of imagination.

Moreover, I was learning that no amount of worrying changes anything except my stomach. Someone has said, "Don't worry about the world ending today. It's already tomorrow in Australia." Instead of giving in to such frustration, I was trying to apply myself to make changes, trusting in God's providence for the outcome, and letting go everything else. I was learning to say, "God, that's your problem, not mine," but at other times, I kept the problem, guarding it as a prize of self-pity.

Finally, years earlier my pastor made a statement I've never forgotten: if we doubt God's love for us, Satan can lead us around by the nose to do his will freely. Though internally at times I felt dead and was angry, yet intellectually I knew that

> I have been crucified with Christ; it is no longer I
> who live, but Christ lives in me; and the *life* which I now
> live in the flesh I live by faith in the Son of God, who
> loved me and gave Himself for me (Galatians 2:20).

Moreover, I kept pounding the doors of heaven, demanding that God do things my way, then one day I came across this verse:

> He gave them their request, but sent leanness into
> their soul (Psalm 106:15).

I backed off and stopped trying to force God's providential hand.

How had the Old Testament saint Job responded when he lost his wealth and his children?

> The LORD gave, and the LORD has taken away;
> blessed be the name of the LORD (Job 1:21).

Mee-Maw said those same words when the news came that her son Thomas had been killed in WWII. Even more to the point, how had the Lord Jesus responded when the Father directed Him to the cross? In the garden just before His crucifixion, He had prayed with sweat that were drops of blood that the cup of the cross be removed, "nevertheless, not as I will, but as You will" He said to God the Father in prayer (Matthew 26:39).

I heard the words, but the pain was still there. Indeed, from those two passages, I learned that it is not wrong to experience the pain, the hurt, and the rejection, as the Lord had felt, but that it is wrong to stop using the means of grace, such as prayer, worship, and doing all that we can to rectify the situation. My grandfather had about 40 cows, and out of that small herd were about five who would always lean against the fence to eat grass on the other side, even though the grass there was worse. We were perpetually repairing fences. We all have a tendency to run to greener pastures, but if we go there, we may find bitter grass. The problem is really not so much the pastures as it is the "cows." Indeed, sometimes we do not want to be around Christians we know because we don't want to be reminded of our pain, we don't want their exhortations, their encouragement, or even their presence. We want to be alone to enjoy our sorrow, but that is

wrong, for we are "not [to forsake] the assembling of ourselves together" (Hebrews 10:25). The Lord's Day is meant to be a time for
renewal. If we begin to drift away from His worship, it becomes easier
not to return.

## Relief

The Lord, however, began to bless the brochures for the carpet company, and in a matter of months the business had increased by 40%.
We hired seminary students to put out the flyers while Richard and I
measured and sold carpet. Business was booming. In April 1982 my
grandmother gave me money to buy into the business; it was her
suggestion as it never entered my mind, so I became a thirty percent
partner. I was making more money that I ever had, but in time my
heart ached for the ministry. When I had hit the bottom, the Lord had
faithfully picked me up, giving me the best job I ever had and with
my best friend, Richard. It was a wonderful few years. But He let me
suffer enough pain so that I was cured of chasing diamond type
schemes. He was gently—and perhaps not so gently but always with
love (Heb. 12:6)—guiding me back into the ministry. **His timing was
slow, it seemed, but that was what it took to get my attention
and to teach me lessons that I've never forgotten**. The next several years in the floor covering business were good ones. I made a de-
cent living, took vacations with the family, and had profitable part
time ministry for five years in Atoka, TN.

I bought a nice house in Mississippi across the pond from my
new business partner, with 3.5 acres. The kids fished and chased
ducks in the pond, and life was good. God had taken me through
four very difficult trials in one year. **His timing for blessing me
seemed grueling and slow**, but it was His way of making me set priorities, of making me persevere, and making me obey when I did not

want to, though my obedience was too often checkered. No pain, no gain. I had come to a practical understanding of verses spoken of the Incarnate Son of God, who was and is God:

> Who, in the days of His flesh, when He had offered
> up prayers and supplications, with vehement cries and
> tears to Him who was able to save Him from death, and
> was heard because of His godly fear, **though He was a
> Son, yet He learned obedience by the things
> which He suffered** (Heb. 5:7-8).

The bold words had puzzled me for years. How could a perfect Son *learn* obedience? He had it by definition. The theological answer was that He was also human; and though as a man He never sinned, He matured (Luke 2:52), and learned *to keep from sinning* by suffering. I concluded, therefore, if the Father's sinless Son suffered and thus learned continued obedience from such, why should I, a sinful human, complain about the same?

We want trials to be over quickly, but the *length* of the trial and the *intensity* of the trial are part of what makes it a trial. We want it to end quickly, Christ says "No," and we learn perseverance (James 1:2-4). We pray for the intensity to ease, Christ says "No," and we learn dependence. **The timing,** therefore, is not just counting hours or days (quantity) but also includes the intensity (quality).

## New Problems

Then in 1986, the Mississippi sale tax authorities went after my partner, Richard, threatening to take his house on a technicality. He sold his house and moved to TN. Then he decided to move to Arkansas (July 1987) where his parents were, and he graciously offered to give me the carpet business. By this time, the business was in financial trouble, and we lost our house and moved back to Memphis. It was a VA loan, and we owed about $20,000, and after other fees, $25,000. VA kept trying to collect it, but I kept telling them I just did not have it. I always answered their letters and phone calls. Then out of the blue, I received a letter from VA offering me a settlement of $10,000, but I still did not have the money. It was the Fall of 1993.

Moreover, the business was a sole proprietorship, build solely around Richard, which did not exist in the abstract. Besides, I was ready to get back into full time ministry. I resigned from the Presbyterian church in Atoka, TN, moved back to Memphis from Mississippi, and went back to the Presbyterian church that I had helped to start in 1979, and this time as a full time minister. It had grown under the able ministry of Dan Morse (now Bp. Morse in the Reformed Episcopal Church). We served together five years as ministers of Grace Presbyterian Church (1986-1991) and then five years when it became Immanuel Reformed Episcopal Church (1991-1996). We took it to almost 200 people, and then I was called to a church in Amarillo. I've been stable in full time Christian work since 1986, and in the REC since May 1991.

# Chapter 11: Arrested by the Feds

The phone rang; it was Susan Sanders calling my wife Ruth. The date was January 9th, 1990, Tuesday, 7 A.M. I was getting ready to begin our home school with 18 students we had gained from various people.

"Ruth, can you come stay with our seven kids. Franklin and I are being arrested, but we can't leave until our children are secured."

The voice was calm and words spoken matter of fact, for Franklin and Susan had expected as much for many months. A half-dozen cars and a dozen officers with automatic weapons had raced up their long driveway in the country, and they stormed the house to subdue this "dangerous" couple with seven home schooled children. It seemed surreal.

Susan calmly opened the door, greeted the IRS CID (Criminal Investigation Division) agent whom they had come to know on a first name basis: "Good morning Bill. As you can see we are about to have breakfast. Care to join us?"

"You and Franklin are under arrest."

"I know, but we must have someone watch our children before we can leave." Bill understood that, and so waited for her to call someone.

As mentioned, she called Ruth, but Ruth had to work. Ruth called Mary Denison to find out where they were working that day. While Ruth talked to Mary, there was a loud pounding on her door, and then on ours. We were all being arrested simultaneously. Months prior to this the others had been told they were under investigation, but I was never told. Ruth was never charged.

The pounding at our front door was so hard that the whole door rattled. We were renting a house, and the front door did not work. Amid much screaming, "Federal agents, open the door, we have an arrest warrant for Mr. Crenshaw," Ruth finally got the arresting officers to understand they needed to enter through the car port as the front door would not open. We did not think about it then, but on the carport door we had two yellow signs that read, "Insured by Smith and Wesson," and "Protected by a pit bull with AIDS." Rocky, our lop-eared pit bull, was on a chain in the back yard. They entered, Ruth said, with guns drawn, demanding:

"Where is Mr. Crenshaw. We have a warrant for his arrest."

She pointed them to the master bedroom where I was dressing, but still in my underwear. I had heard them. They yelled out:

"Mr. Crenshaw!"

"Yes."

"Mr. Crenshaw!"

"Yes."

"Mr. Crenshaw!"

"Yes."

(Three times; I guess they were slow that morning.)

"You're under arrest. Come out with your hands up."

"I'm coming out."

"You're hands better be up."

"They're up."

So I stepped into the hall. Across the hall were the bedrooms of my son and daughter. They asked:

"Do you want the doors of your children shut?"

I answered emphatically: "No." I wanted witnesses in case they abused their authority and for our children to see what could happen when government was misled.

As I stepped into the hall, one gun was pushed into my stomach and another put to my head.

Obviously with only underwear on, I did not need to be searched. I calmly told them I would cooperate with whatever they wanted me to do, at which point they became completely calm, put their guns away, repeated what I had said to the other officers, ask me if I had any guns in the house, and then read me my rights, and in that order. While I dressed in my bedroom, one officer accompanied me. (They should have read the rights before asking me questions.)

At first they were extremely nervous, and we concluded later that the prosecuting woman, "Debra," had told them we (all 26 people arrested that morning) were very dangerous people. They came to my house with three cars, two arresting officers per car. As they took me to the den, I saw through a window two of those officers playing with our wimpy pit bull in the back yard! He was licking them. (Surely I must have been dangerous with a pit bull!) These officers were from out of town so I had to direct them downtown to the federal build-ing. They treated me courteously, loosing my handcuffs to make them comfortable as they drove me.

The agreement my attorney had with the government was that if I were indicted, they would call him, and I could walk in. I had re-tained the attorney as a caution, but I had never been told that I was under investigation. They arrested me at gunpoint. Did they forget or just want their pound of flesh?

Once inside the house, a woman arresting officer kept asking Ruth if I had a computer or guns, but Ruth would (deliberately) go into a crying fit, so they never made progress with that. They wanted everyone's computer. Of course, my computer only had sermons and theological writings, but it would have put me out of business for a while, which was probably the intent. If they had entered through the front door, they would have seen my computer, but at the time we did not think of any of that.

They confiscated the computers of everyone they could, and I wondered if they had warrants for them. Twenty-six were arrested, 11 from our church, and 18 went to trial. There were 47 felony counts against those who went to trial. The other eight had plea bargained, which is what they expected us in the church to do. They never used any evidence from any computer (that I can remember) because there wasn't any! We were really engaged in ministry, not government conspiracies.

I learned how the system worked. Don't think that someone is necessarily guilty if they plea bargain, because the way the "game" is played is that the prosecution tells you that you don't have a chance, what you are facing, how many years you'll get, they can even legally lie to you, and once you're scared witless, then you'll say, do, and sign anything. You'll testify falsely in court to save yourself. Guilty people plea bargain; scared people plea bargain; innocent people don't. We didn't. On one occasion before the trial, the prosecution and main investigator ganged up on my friend Richard and tried to scare him into lying for them, but it did not work. He feared God more than man.

Once we got downtown, we entered the federal building from the basement. Michael Osborne, a close friend and church member, was standing on a concrete platform with a jogging suit on. (He has preceded me into the presence of the sovereign Lord and my heart still aches to see him. We rode together to the trial, along with the Sanders, for those 4 ½ months that we were forced to watch the wicked outsmart themselves in court). He was standing there hand-cuffed with his arms behind his back, and he said to me crisply, as if we were meeting to have breakfast at Shoney's, "Good morning." I responded in kind.

We were processed, taken before a magistrate who negotiated our bond. Mine was set for $25,000, higher than rapists and murderers. The main target, Franklin Sanders, had a bond of $100,000. My attorney, whom I had retained several months before, met me in court, and had my bail lowered to $10,000. Later that evening when I got home, I saw on the news that someone who was charged with rape had his bail set at $10,000. I had to put up ten percent or $1,000. Because we confessed Jesus as Lord over the government, we were more dangerous than rapists and murderers who were a threat only to those they assaulted.

With my one phone call, I told Ruth to take some cash we rarely had, but on this providential day did, and go see a certain bondsman my attorney recommended. I had to make bail by 5 pm or spend the night in jail; I made bail at 4:55 pm. **God's timing was encouraging,** and I went home to a sleepless night. Many of those arrested spent several nights in jail until they could make bail.

So what were we charged with? Here is the language from the indictment that we had allegedly conspired to

> "defraud the U.S. by impeding, impairing, destructing, and defeating the lawful Government functions of the IRS of the Treasury Department in the ascertainment, computation, assessment, and collection of revenue, that is, taxes. . . ."

Other charges were similarly worded. But it was more than taxes. The fact that they went after church records, and not just financial records, indicated that this was a church-state conflict. They did not believe we were a legitimate church, but they had no evidence to the contrary, and our denomination headquarters, the Presbyterian Church in America in the summer of 1989, sent a letter of protest to the D.A., saying we were a legitimate church in good standing with one of the largest denominations in the USA.

A few in our church were charged with willful failure to file an income tax return. Some, to this day, think that it is a crime not to file one, but that is a common misunderstanding. (Interestingly, it is only a misdemeanor not to file if required, but a felony to file fraudulently.) First, one must have enough income to be required to file. Second, to be a crime and not a mistake, one must have been required to file by not only having enough income, but must have known that, and must have refused to do so willfully. Those few in our congregation who had not filed, had not done so with the idea of disobeying the law; indeed, they wanted to obey the law. The dispute with them was what the law said. They were trying to ask the government for elaboration, but the government refused to answer.

We had to put up with incredible ignorance and acrimony from those Christians who thought we must be guilty of something, and who refused to listen to our explanations. Even recently one person said to me: "You know that some in your church were guilty of something." The Bible calls that bearing false witness, and that person apparently does not believe that Caesar arrests innocent people.

What did the government want? They wanted to discredit our local church, to shut it down, to silence those in the congregation who were outspoken against some government taxes, and against other government abuses, like abortion, against paper money (the Constitution specifically requires our money to be backed by silver and gold), and we opposed such ideas as having a government program for every human need, as if the government were God who would "give us this day, our daily bread." Who was it who said, "For every action there is an equal and opposite government program"? Moreover, several of our attorneys stated that the government wanted to set a precedent, for if it could run over the rights and get all the records of a small church in a large denomination, they would use that precedent to do the same for larger churches and other denominations.

Before the trial began, Dan Morse met with the woman prosecutor and the IRS investigator, along with the church's attorney, who stated regarding those two government employees: "In my many years of practice, I have not run into two government agents who have so completely lost objectivity and are determined to twist everything to fit their preconceptions" (Quoted from Dan Morse's upcoming book on the trial, title to be determined.)

So was there a conspiracy? Yes, the government engaged in a conspiracy to run over the rights of individuals and of a small church, challenging Christ that He could not protect us. They plotted a vain thing and thought they could overthrow the purpose of Christ and thwart His rule by their machinations, but the Lord Jesus had something to say about that. (You must read Psalm 2:1-4.)

The church continued to support Dan and me financially during the 4 ½ months we were in court as if nothing had happened. Indeed, we continued our ministries, deliberately ignoring the government trial as much as we could. The female judge said we should take the trial very, very seriously as this was the most significant thing that had ever happened to us. We refused to accept that.

## Embarrassment

We had been telling our presbytery about the government investigating our church for months. During one special presbytery meeting called by the Minister's Committee in late 1989, they asked that we bring the church's attorney at our expense to explain what was going on. The attorney lived a considerable distance. The presbytery thought that our church had called the special meeting and that we were trying to force an issue. The Minister's Committee did not speak up to say they requested us to bring in the church's attorney. Thus, one arrogant minister made a motion that our attorney not be allowed to speak! To show how angry the presbytery was at us, they voted to sustain the motion. Thus, our lawyer was flown in, and our church paid him for nothing. The presbytery did not want to come to our aid or to listen to the story and stand with us. They abandoned us, across the board, with perhaps one exception, but he never contacted us or tried to encourage us.

Once we were arrested and made the news on TV and in the paper, our presbytery wanted to distance itself from us. Thus, they called a special meeting of the presbytery to deal with us, ordered an investigation of Dan and me, even wanting to see our IRS tax returns! That was ridiculous to think that after the government had investigated us that Presbytery would do so again, and of course any documents we would turn over to them could be subpoenaed by the government, which they would have turned over without considering the crown rights of the King of kings. It was also most unloving to kick us while we were down. Almost half the presbytery, at a subsequent meeting, wanted Dan and me to resign from the ministry. To both the documents and resigning, Dan and I said a strong "No." Contrary to our Book of Church Order and to the Bible, they were considering us guilty until proven innocent. One very arrogant and angry lay person, we'll call "Bob," said to the presbytery: "The government has better things to do than to go around arresting innocent people." "Bob" was appointed to the committee to investigate us.

During the 4 ½ months of our trial, four to five days a week, eight hours a day, only one person from the presbytery came to our trial. He had voted against us in presbytery. The trial had been in progress about a month when he came. David said:

"I'm astonished at the bias of the judge, and if I had known more of your situation, I would have voted for y'all."

I responded: "You did know because we told you. Besides, you violated the Bible and our own church standards in considering us guilty of some crime without a trial."

Bonhoeffer's woes with his Lutheran "brethren" come to mind, as they abandoned him. He was hanged eleven days before the Allies delivered Germany from Hitler. Like him, we had been abandoned to the government by our own presbytery and by virtually every minister in the city. We were alone, almost. Of course, the Lord had not abandoned us.

There were a few who stood with us. One couple from out of town, came numerous times to the trial. They would stay in a motel for a week at a time, be in court, pray, and encourage us. The first time they were there, they noted the bias, manipulation, and demonic atmosphere in the court without us having to point it out. That is the only way to describe it. Virtually everything the prosecutor wanted, the judge gave her. There were times (very few) when the judge was very emphatic about a point against the government; but when "Debra" would not back down, the judge would capitulate—almost every time. Not only this, but when "Debra" was present, the demeanor of the court room was oppressing, the judge full of ranker, and it felt like a dark cloud was in the court room.

But there was one other significant person who stood with us. With all the double standards of the PCA, Dan and I and the elders of our Presbyterian church were looking for another denomination. We had heard that Ray Sutton had joined the REC, Reformed Episcopal Church. Bishop Roy Grote came to see us about possibly joining. He looked over our financial records (as would be appropriate even if we were not on trial), talked with us, and stood with us during the trial. Finally, we had a pastor who loved us and considered us innocent of any crimes until proved guilty. In May 1991, Dan and I flew to New Providence, NJ to be examined with a view to being accepted as ministers in the REC; we both were. The next month our whole church voted to transfer into the REC, minus one family that wanted to remain Presbyterian. We had about 180 members at that time. After 21 years and counting, I'm still waiting to have an argument on the floor of our "presbytery," which we call a "diocese." I had come home and that to a pastoral model from a confrontational model. I've had stable ministry for these 21 years.

All through the trial, Dan and I wore clerical attire, even as Presbyterians. We wanted the authority of the Church to be felt in court.

# Chapter 12: God's "Deck" Was Stacked

**M**any times at our Church we prayed that the Lord Jesus would grant us victory in such a way that it would be obvious that He was the one who did it, not us. Indeed, that is just what happened. Here are the details as I recall them and from my diary.

To me, the Sovereign King's gracious providence during the trial was like a card game I had played. My grandparents and I would play a game they called "Pitch." Once when I was about 19, I stacked the deck before they came to the table to play. One had to bid on a certain suit (diamonds, spades, etc) if he wanted that suit to act as trump. If one did not make his bid, he would go backwards that many points. No one questioned the deck, for I told them I had shuffled it. My grandfather bid three points, which normally was enough to win the bid and set which suit would be trump. My grandmother, with a wide smile, bid four, which was rare. I bid five. The most points one could make in a game was six, and my grandfather said with eager voice, "That boy's going set," which meant I would not make the bid and would go in the hole five points.

We had one opportunity to throw away our cards that were not the right suit and ask for more. There were only six cards each one drew at the beginning. My grandfather asked for three, my grandmother three, and I asked for five. By the way I had the deck stacked, I knew how many each would draw, what they would draw, that I would draw five, and what those five would be. My grandfather just laughed and said I was quite the gambler. As we laid down our cards six times, at first it looked bad for me, but when the last card was played, I won it all—six points. My grandfather smelled a rat, so I told them what I had done. From then on when we began to play, my grandfather would cut the deck! Likewise, for 4 ½ months in court we lost motions, legal briefs, points of law, and it seemed the trial was going against us at every point, but the last hand had not been played.

## Court Appointed Attorneys

To get a court appointed attorney we had to take the stand and under oath reveal our financial position. Yet the trial was about money, so how would we do this? I never agonized over anything as much as I did this. For days I tried to figure out what to do. I could not get an attorney without revealing my financial position; and if I did this, they could use the information I gave them against me, even though there was very little money I had to worry about. We had several defendants who could afford their own attorney.

Finally, I decided to take the stand and let the chips fall where they may. I never prayed harder over anything. When the day came for me to appear before the magistrate, my stomach was in knots. Church member Mark Denison was the first to stand up.

"Your honor, I and many others here have a dilemma. As I understand it, I need to disclose my finances to prove that I cannot afford an attorney, but the trial is about my finances. What am I to do?"

Magistrate Allen: "You only need to state under oath that you cannot afford an attorney, and one will be appointed to you. At the end of the trial, you may have to disclose your financial position."

A huge weight suddenly evaporated! Magistrate Allen appointed anyone an attorney who could say he did not want to reveal his finances and yet could not afford one. As it turned out, at the end of the trial nothing was ever said about disclosing our finances, for such was done for everyone in the course of the trial when the government gave its evidence.

So what kind of attorneys did we get? They were excellent, to a person. I had been told that court appointed attorneys could not make it in private practice so they got on the government trial list. They would hold your hand while you went to jail. But every one of our attorneys—both men and women—had many years of experience. They were chosen at random off a court list—like casting the dice—but its every decision was from the Lord (Prov. 16:33)!

The attorney God gave me was Alan Bryant Chambers, a man with 20 years experience in criminal law. (He had successfully defended my cousin who had been fired by Reagan when all the air traffic controllers had gone on strike. He was actually sick at home, not pretending.) Alan was also very conscious of his demeanor and his presence before the court and the jury. He often did all he could to keep from offending the judge, the jury, and other defendants. He described himself as an agnostic Roman Catholic, and he was well read in church history.

The other defendants could echo what I've said about their court appointed attorneys. Susan Sanders had Ed Chandler. Though he was also an agnostic, he defended her with great zeal and knowledge. On opening statements, Chandler came out of the gate like a bull at the rodeo, arguing with high decibels her innocence before the jury. The judge did not like his demeanor and called him down on several occasions for being too forceful. Michael Osborne's young daughter was there for the opening statement, and she summed up Chandler's demeanor best: "Mommy, he keeps saying 'Yes ma'am' to the judge, but he does what he wants." One thing all the court appointed attor-

neys stated was that we were not like most of their clients: drug deal-
ers, murderers, and liars. We were respectable, sincere, God-fearing,
non-violent people who loved their country. When the attorneys saw
who we were, they became very enthusiastic and the trial became
personal—they wanted to win, for *us*.

## The Mystery of Providence

God stacks the deck of life in favor of His people, though sometimes
it may seem that we have lost if the Great Shepherd of the sheep allows the enemy to gain temporary victory, even allowing his sheep to
be killed—but they go home, so they win even then.

We defendants tried several times to have separate trials, but the
judge absolutely refused. That meant we must all be tried together,
for they were counting on guilt by association.

There was a lead defense attorney who was exceptionally good
at cross examination, and we were able to raise money to retain him
for one of our co-defendants. How did that happen? The Lord of glory stacked the deck.

The government had over 100 witnesses who took the stand
against us, but the jury later said they contradicted one another and
exonerated us at times with their details. How did that happen? The
Lord of glory stacked the deck.

Their first witness was a former disgruntled member of our
church who played Judas against me and others. After one rather obvious time of lying on the stand, at a morning break one of our
church members, who was observing the trial, asked him, "How many
pieces of silver did you get for that?" That was an obvious reference
to Judas who received 30 pieces of silver to betray Jesus. Though I
harbor no animosity in my heart against him, it was an appropriate
question.

## Choosing of the Jury

But to me the **most remarkable providence of all was the choosing of the jury**. About 100 potential jurors were brought into the courtroom. Their names were written on 3 x 5 cards, then placed in a circular box in the front of the court, the box was turned with a handle to tumble the cards, and the court clerk would look away and pull out a card. As the name was called, the potential juror would walk from the back of the courtroom to the juror's box. Then came the questions we had submitted to the judge to ask. We wanted Christian jurors; the government was so sure of its case, they did not care. After each potential juror had been questioned, we exited to a witness room that could barely hold 18 defendants and attorneys. On more than one occasion, I can still see Franklin, the main target of the trial, with his tall stature snapping his fingers high in the air amid all the confusion and talking loudly, "Hold it, hold it, let's all get together, we need to hear one another." Out of all that chaos, after rejecting all the jurors we were allowed to reject except one, we had a jury of 15. Twelve would be the jury, but in case some had to leave for whatever reason, we would not have to try the case again for want of jurors.

Consider the diversity of the jury: black, white, male, female, young, old, working, and retired. I recall one older man with a poker face who chewed gum the whole trial. Since he was older, my concern was that he would be against alleged conspirators who were allegedly trying to keep the government from rightful taxes, which meant we did not want him to have his Social Security check. All that was false, as the jury came to understand. Later, we discovered he was a member of the John Birch Society (!), an organization that believes in government conspiracies against its citizens. Then the jury foreman was an airline pilot who was out of work for the time, and an evangelical Christian.

The government was so confident of its case that it had not rejected a single juror during the selecting process. Who could think that there was a God so sovereign that He could stack the deck so that even though "the lot is cast into the lap, its every decision is from the LORD" (Proverbs 16:33)? That never entered the prosecution's mind; it did ours, and we prayed hard for months, read the Psalms, and called on the Name of the Lord to be pleased to deliver us. So the jury was chosen by lot—and by providence.

The last defense we have against tyranny is the jury. Judges will often not allow Constitutional argument in the courts as these are deemed "irrelevant." Grand Juries are nothing more than rubber stamps for prosecutors. Congress pays little attention to the Constitution; neither does the Supreme Court, it seems at times. But the local jury is the last stronghold against tyranny in this nation.

Most jurors do not know that they are judges not only of the facts but also of the law. Our judge vehemently denied this. If juries are not judges of the law, then we are subject to the whims of tyrants and whatever laws they want to shove down our throats. (Such is how we should understand the Magna Carta of 1215.) She would not hear of this but constantly maintained that the jury was duty bound to honor the law *as she would give it* to them at the end of the trial. Of course some other judge would give a different version of the law. As one man well stated: "We used to have laws, now we have judges." The Tennessee Constitution states that juries are judges of both the facts *and the law.* ". . . the jury shall have a right to determine the law and the facts, under the direction of the court, as in other criminal cases" (Article I, Section 19).

## When the Trial Began

As I mentioned earlier, we were arrested on Tuesday morning, January 9th, 1990. (My father died the following Sunday.) The judge wanted the trial to begin in September, then October, and finally she set a date in November that she would **not bend on**. She was not in charge, however, the Triune God was, and the trial was delayed until the latter part of February, 1991. **The significance of the timing** is that the Supreme Court ruled in the Cheek case in January, shortly before our trial began, that defendants should be allowed to argue the legal cases that they relied on in forming their legal positions. Our judge understood this to mean that defendants could make the argument but that they were still not allowed to actually have the cases in their hands in court. Then there was another ruling that helped us just prior to the defense beginning their part of the case in June 1991. The Powell case in the Ninth Circuit Court of Appeals, stated that defendants must be allowed to use the cases—in court, written out, entered into evidence—that they had relied on. God was gracious to us in this **critical timing** to make changes in the understanding of the law in our favor. We could all argue the law and enter the law into evidence.

In other words, a defendant could be found not guilty if he sincerely believed that he was obeying the law as he understood it, even if he had broken the law. To be found guilty of a tax violation, one must be guilty of *knowingly* and *willingly* breaking the law. The two cases helped a minority of the defense. Sincerely misunderstanding the tax law was a good defense against criminal charges, though not against civil charges, paying taxes.

# Chapter 13: Collusion and Bias?

The judge constantly criticized the defense to maintain a neutral face in the presence of the jury. Yet she had one of the most expressive faces I had ever seen, and could be quite charming when she wanted to be. I wrote many times in my notes the way the judge would make faces that betrayed her attitude. For example, she would frown when she did not like what the defense said. She would raise her eyebrows in her "now little children" manner when she wanted to communicate her disgust against the defense. She would wave her hand in gesture to the prosecution that it was time to object. She would put her hand over her forehead and look down when she thought the defense did something stupid, sometimes wagging her head back and forth. She *never* did these things to the prosecution, *not once*.

There were times when the judge could be very articulate, and she had an almost photographic memory for details. But when she would scold the defense, she would often ramble on until our ears were drooping. She had the rare ability to compress the most words into the smallest idea.

One example of her bias was regarding Lloyd Bauer, a convert to the Lord from Mormonism and a member of our church. The judge ruled that a tape recording of one of Lloyd Bauer's meetings could be brought in as evidence and that this was not a First Amendment issue. I almost dropped my jaw. Lloyd Bauer had public meetings on the Constitution, a First Amendment right if there ever was one, and yet this had nothing to do with the First Amendment! Two IRS special agents ("Nancy" and "Bob") had lied to Lloyd about their identity and secretly taped his meeting. The meetings were public and protected under the freedom of speech Amendment, but the judge ruled against the Bauers anyway. When it was pointed out that the taping by "Nancy" and "Bob" was contrary to the Special Agents Handbook, the judge ruled that the IRS did not have to follow their own handbook!

One humorous question by Mr. Bauer was to agent "Nancy" on cross examination, who had actually done the taping. She had gone to the rest room to turn the tape over and had flushed the toilet, which had been recorded. Lloyd asked:

"When we heard the flushing, was that you flushing the First Amendment down the toilet?"

The judge got *extremely* angry, sending the jury out so she could blast Lloyd. Everyone else laughed hard, including the jury.

On another occasion, "Nancy" had lied to Lloyd Bauer about her name, pretending to be "Bob's" wife. Both "Nancy" and "Bob" were special investigators for the IRS. A "special" investigator is with the criminal part of the IRS, not the auditor that most people are familiar with. The special agent puts you in jail; the auditor takes your money.

When "Nancy" took the stand, she had an excellent memory for the government; but when we cross examined her, she constantly said "I can't recall." We wondered if the jury believed her. Another IRS witness, Mrs. "Bragg," constantly said to the defense on cross examination: "I don't recall." "I don't understand your question." When she did answer, she stated things differently from the way the question was worded, making the listeners wonder what she meant by the answer. These kinds of responses were typical of the government's witnesses, and we wondered if the jury was seeing through such antics.

There were tense moments during the trial, usually caused by the judge's bias. On April 9, 1991 Howard Bruner, who was with the CSX Railroad, was testifying against Jim Hollingsworth, a member of our church. He was making statements about the law when the government was asking him questions on direct testimony. Now the judge had not allowed anyone to say anything about the law during the trial. Repeatedly she kept saying that she would instruct the jury about the law at the end of the trial. The jury was supposed to judge the facts—not the law.

But on this occasion, the judge was allowing the witness to give testimony about the law, and it was essentially the same interpretation that the judge held, which may be the reason she allowed it. Defense attorney Jeff Dickstein stood up and said to the judge that if she allowed testimony about the law that he should have the right to cross examine on the law. Everyone took the judge's silence to mean that she agreed.

When it came time for cross examination of the witness, Mr. Dickstein, being one of the first attorneys to cross and being the best one at both cross examination and in understanding the law, began to ask the witness questions about the law. The prosecution objected, and the judge sustained it. Now one rule in courts is that the opposing attorneys get to ask questions on the topic that the original attorney questioned in direct examination. How could the prosecution object to this? Mr. Dickstein pursued another angle along the same line. Again the prosecution objected and again the judge sustained.

After this happened several times, most of the defense attorneys simultaneously rose and in clear, forceful terms strongly objected, such as Larry Beacraft, Ed Chandler, Seabiert, my attorney Alan

Chambers, Boyd, and others. This infuriated the judge, and she told everyone in no uncertain terms that she was in charge.

About this time Lloyd Bauer, who was seated up front close to the judge because he had a hearing problem, could take it no longer and he stood up, pointed to jurors seated in their box, and yelled—and I do mean *yelled*—to the judge.

"Why don't you dismiss the jury and have a sentencing hearing because you're not interested in having the jury hear the truth."

As Lloyd spoke of the jury, he pointed his long finger at the jury, and as he spoke of the judge, he pointed at her. The judge began to shake and her voice quaked. She sent the jury out and went into tirade number one thousand. She threatened to send Lloyd to jail if he did anything like that again. Then she jumped on all the attorneys who had jumped up and objected, which is to say she castigated them for doing their job. My attorney, who always seemed to have the balance between tact and attacking, and who rarely said anything, stated forcefully (I have the wording in my notes):

"My ability to represent Mr. Crenshaw is being chilled [legal language], for if I have to discern subjectively when I will be allowed to object, reading your silence, how can I represent my client?"

By "silence" he meant how to interpret the judge's silence to Dickstein's request to be able to cross on the law.

The judge gave us an extended break to "cool down." She had royally blown it, but pride kept her from saying so.

## Church's Records

Late in the trial, the government asked the judge to order the church to give over its financial records, which we objected to on the grounds of separation of church and state, but we were willing to do so as far as having nothing to hide and if the records were only financial ones. But the judge wanted them all, including counseling records and internal records of the operation of the church. Thus, we had to stop the trial to deal with that matter, and the church had to hire its own attorney to represent it. The fateful day came when the church's attorney appeared in court.

The judge: "Mr. 'Jones' (not real name), do you have the records I ordered you to bring?"

"Judge, we must insist that specific records be named, and not allow a fishing expedition."

"Are the records in your possession?"

"Yes, judge."

"Are they with you today?"

"No, your honor."

"Well, why not?"

"The church has consistently asked for over a year that the demand be of financial records, not all the records of the church, which would include private counseling records."

"Then I shall have a hearing to determine if you're in contempt of court."

"Your honor, I have a right to counsel."

The church's attorney, a Christian man, now needed an attorney, and we brought in one of the best in the country, Edwin Vieira. He was a conservative Roman Catholic, from Washington, D.C., and specialized in appeal cases and Constitutional law. He was a powerhouse, quoting Supreme Court cases rapidly to the judge from memory like a machine gun. He told us later that our case was being watched carefully from Washington, and the government wanted to make an example of us.

Moreover, the elders and pastors of the church were all willing to go to jail over this issue of the government lording it over the church. Giving the judge financial records was one thing, but allowing her to go on a fishing expedition through all the records of the church, was another. We would not back down.

At this point, the judge was trumped. The trial could have been delayed for weeks, if not months, while we appealed her ruling, and we had an issue that could blow the case up. Her ruling was a highly appealable issue, and no judge likes to have her cases overturned. So she finally consented. We gave her the church's cancelled checks, treasurer reports, and I'm not sure what else, but no private counseling records and no records of the internal working of the church. Out of hundreds of documents, she turned over only two financial items (!) to the prosecution, both pertaining to me: a voided check (!) made out to me, and a check made out to my little publishing venture, Footstool Publications, for about $500, a gift from the church to publish books. I truly hope she was embarrassed.

## Witnesses Against Me

Throughout the course of the trial, the only witness who said anything bad about me was the one lying witness at the beginning of the trial, who manufactured details against many of the defendants, apparently to save himself from what he thought would be charges. He had been a former member of our church. When I returned to the church, he was a member, and he left shortly after I arrived so I had only known him a few months. I had helped him and his wife through the death of their baby, and his response was to lie against me in open court.

The government subpoenaed Bilbo Gatlin, an elder at a church I had been pastor of some years prior. The government wanted to show that I allegedly had income that I had not reported so they had him bring church records where they had paid me. I had already told the church to be prepared to do this several years prior to the trial. When my attorney asked Mr. Gatlin about my ministry, he stated:

"Rev. Crenshaw indeed preached the Gospel. He worked hard for what he was paid; I received what I paid for; namely, a pastor who faithfully ministered to me and the people and who taught the Word." He mentioned that I had traveled 52 miles each way to church.

Another witness that was called to testify against me, but like Mr. Gatlin really testified for me, was George Calhoun. (The government paid his way and expenses to testify, and he ended up being my witness!) I had done some computer work for him in Mt. Olive, MS at the Mt. Olive Tape Library of Reformed Theology, and the government wanted to show that I had income I had not allegedly reported. According to my notes, Mr. Calhoun stated:

"Mr. Crenshaw did some computer work for the Mt. Olive Tape Library, and I had to force him to take some money for expenses; otherwise, he would have done it free. If the truth were known, I owe Mr. Crenshaw $5,000 for his work, but was not able to pay him." (And he said many other such kind words.)

Everyone was in tears over Mr. Calhoun's testimony, including some in the jury, not only what he said about me, but because he was an old man who could hardly walk even using a cane, obviously sick, who could hardly talk, and yet the government made him come from 300 miles away, stay two nights in a motel, to testify against me and did not treat him with respect. He was distinguished looking with his white hair. When Mr. Calhoun first took the stand, it took him several minutes to walk to the stand because of his health. Yet the prosecution, now "Tom" since "Debra" was in the hospital with ulcerated colitis, bluntly demanded that he speak up. Mr. Calhoun responded very slowly and in measured words:

"Sir, I have pulmonary fibrosis and I'm doing the best I can."

As we were leaving court that day, I said to Dan Morse: "They shot themselves in the foot with Mr. Calhoun."

He responded: "Wrong. They shot themselves in both feet and the head."

When it came time to give the case to the jury, the judge gave instructions about the law and that they should view us defendants as innocent until proved beyond a reasonable doubt. I thought she did a good job, and for once was fair, and balanced. Moreover, she said no defendant was required to take the stand, and if one had not, that was no presumption of guilt.

# Chapter 14: The Verdicts Were Read

The prosecution had all the time they wanted to try their case, three and a half months, four to five days a week, six to seven hours a day, but the defense was constantly harassed by the judge to get done, giving us less than a month. Finally, on July 8th, a Monday morning, the trial was given to the jury to decide. We sat around and waited for God's providence.

At one court break about two months before our trial was over, the lead investigator of all the defendants said to one of the defense attorneys, shaking his head with a smug look on his face: "Oh yeah, we win 99% of these type conspiracy cases."

Then around noon the next day, Tuesday, we were told we had a verdict. To come back that fast with verdicts for so many defendants with so many counts meant either very good news or very bad news. There were now 17 defendants and 46 counts. One lady had made a deal, pleading guilty to a misdemeanor if she would not go to jail, to be with her children if her husband went to jail for a felony, which was a very gracious thing to do, even though she was really not guilty. She had been eight months pregnant when arrested. Just before going in to hear the verdicts, Michael Osborne led us all in prayer with something like this:

> "Almighty God our Heavenly Father, regardless of the outcome, we thank you for the opportunity to learn faith, to walk not by sight, but to trust you in the midst of very trying times. We ask your mercy to be on those

who have opposed us. Now give us grace to accept what
you have decided for us."

I'll have to confess there was a part of me that did not like that
prayer, but considering that Michael had the most to lose (something
like 30 years in jail), it sank into my heart with great emotion. Though
I'm sure I don't have the words exact, the impact is still there as I
write this. Now was the time to hear the verdicts.

As we entered the courtroom, I noticed that there were government men on all the back rows where the public would sit, though
the public rarely attended, except for one newspaper reporter and
the couple I mentioned earlier, and a few interested friends or relatives on rare occasions, such as my step-father, who supported us.
My mother could not attend until after she testified for me, which
was very late in the trial. The government men were waiting to arrest
us out of the courtroom, which was almost unheard of, for we should
have at least a month to prepare our case why our sentences should
be light. That further meant the judge had pre-signed orders for our
immediate arrests. The news media were there to help make the final
splash. All the defendants were required to stand. The foreman led
the jury in with a manila file folder that contained all the verdict
forms. He was ordered to walk up front to hand the verdicts to the
court clerk, who in turn gave them to the judge. As she looked at
them, her face turned white.

She handed the verdicts back to the foreman and asked him to
read them. He looked surprised, and said,

"All the verdicts, your honor." She replied "Yes." He said, "For all
counts"? She said, "Yes."

He had to do that for the record, 46 verdicts, one for each count.

As all the defendants and attorneys stood, you could hear a butterfly's wings. For 18 months our lives had been on hold, and our thoughts dominated by the trial, the evidence, and the witnesses. We had not been able to leave town without court approval. If we were sick, we had to have court approval to go to the doctor if it meant missing court. Once when two of Franklin and Susan Sander's sons were burned in an accident, they had been taken to a nearby children's hospital. We heard about it at lunch, and Franklin and Susan, and Dan and I as pastors, went running, literally as it was only a few blocks, to see them. Dan and I made it back in time for court, but Franklin and Susan stayed. The judge was very angry they did not get approval from her, to which Franklin later said, "She would have to kill me to keep me from my sons." Their burns turned out not to be life threatening, but both needed skin grafts.

We defendants, our church, and many friends had prayed our hearts out, had done all we knew to do. The judge had constantly sent the jury out so she could scold the defendants and attorneys, which she never did, *not once* the whole trial, to the prosecution. We wondered if the jury really understood what was going on. Did they see the hypocrisy of the judge and prosecution, their collusion, the judge's many faces, and the inconsistency of the witnesses among themselves and even the inconsistency of one witness from one day to the next? Did they believe our testimony? Had they believed my witnesses and my testimony when I took the stand? If we went to jail, how would our families survive? I loved my nation; I shed my life's blood for the USA in Vietnam, but I was being wrongly accused.

Most of us had dependent children. (Mine were 16 and 12.) If both Dan and I went to jail, would the church survive? The Rev. Coe had not been indicted, and he was a capable man, but the people were used to multiple ministers and multiple ministry. How would my wife and children survive? We had been counting on having a month to make plans for our families if convicted, but many plain clothes government men were there to arrest us immediately, which indicated how vindictive the judge and prosecution were. Was it personal with them? Did they hate us that badly? We had contacted everyone we knew once we received word that the verdicts would be read in an hour or about. It all came down to the next few minutes. Seventeen defendants, attorneys, families, our whole church held their breath. The jury foreman began to read the verdicts, beginning with the most culpable, and the charge everyone had—conspiracy.

"C. Franklin Sanders, concerning the count of conspiracy, (my lungs were suspended) . . . not guilty."

*Immediately,* 17 defendants began to sniffle. I could hardly believe my ears. I was only charged with that one count, and if the center of the alleged conspiracy was not guilty, how could I be in a conspiracy with him? All the other counts against Franklin were read as not guilty. Then his lovely wife with seven children had been charged, which was the most vindictive thing I've ever seen. She was not guilty on all charges.

When the verdicts against Michael Osborne were all not guilty, his sniffling turned to bawling. I can still see him gripping the back of his chair, standing there, head down, shoulders heaving. His attorney next to him grabbed him with a bear hug. Another defendant was not guilty, whom Michael's attorney was friends with, but was some distance away. No matter, his attorney stepped on chairs to get to him, at which point they collapsed into one another's arms.

Now the judge was ordering everyone to be quiet, to no avail. As the not guilty verdicts continued, I was in the last third of the defendants, least culpable, and I turned to my court appointed attorney, who described himself as an agnostic Roman Catholic, and said,

"Allen, did you ever see anything like this?"

He kept shaking his head and saying, "In 21 years of practice, I never thought I'd witness anything like this. I can't understand it."

To which I said with breaking voice, "It's easy, Allen, King Jesus has bared His mighty arm to demonstrate who was in charge all along."

By the time my not guilty verdict was read, defendants were slapping each other, rejoicing, as well as crying. Some in the jury were crying with us; others were smiling. As the not guilty verdicts were being read, I kept looking over my shoulder where the government men had been sitting to arrest us, and they began to peel off the rows like airplanes in formation. By the time the last verdict was read, they were all gone.

Now the judge was beside herself, and could not stand our open joy so she vehemently ordered us to be quiet while the remaining few verdicts were read. The last verdict was of Dale O'Gwen who had spent some time in the outback of Alaska. He had been snowed in on January 9th, 1990, when all the arrests took place, and could not be arrested until spring! Then he had driven himself to Memphis and turned himself in. One night we had a prayer meeting for the upcoming trial, and we were at the Bauers' home. We prayed for Dale, and specifically for his safety in driving from Alaska to Memphis, TN. As soon as we finished, there was a knock at the door. Guess who? Dale. Such a hardened criminal he allegedly was who drove himself all the way from Alaska to turn himself in! (Remember a similar thing happened with Peter in Acts 12:13ff when he was delivered from prison while the disciples prayed. They went to the door, and it was Peter!)

Dale's verdict was last. When it was read, he deliberately stepped to the center of the courtroom, raised both hands toward heaven with fingers extended to receive the blessing, looked up toward the ceiling as if looking into the face of God, and in defiance of the judge's order to be quiet, yelled at the top of his lungs: "PRAISE GOD!" All the defendants spontaneously broke into the doxology with one voice in praise to the Holy Trinity:

> Praise God, from whom all blessings flow;
> Praise Him, all creatures here below;
> Praise Him above, ye heav'nly host;
> Praise Father, Son, and Holy Ghost.

It was obvious to us where the victory had come from. **It was a very last minute deliverance**—the last day of the trial—**but right on time!** I kept record, and still have in my notes, what our percentage was of winning motions in court. The best day we lost 82%, and most days we lost 100%. The government had all the money they wanted to prosecute our case, but we were limited to what we could raise. They had over 100 witnesses. They had entered thousands of documents into evidence, and in some instances they had entered whole boxes of evidence. They had the judge on their side. We had limited funds and less time, but we had the Lord and we won by His grace. The Federal building was near the Mississippi River downtown Memphis, and I was ready to walk on water, right across to Arkansas!

After the last verdict was read, and the judge got control of the courtroom again, she wanted to find a way to retry the case, or so it appeared. She polled the individual jurors whether the verdicts were theirs alone, whether there had been contact with the defendants, whether they had talked among themselves before being given the trial, compromised confidentiality, or were pressured in any way. The jurors, having seen the tyranny of the judge, were expecting her to do that! Each juror was firm that the verdicts were his/hers alone. There was nothing more she could do. *A not guilty verdict in a jury trial in a criminal case cannot be appealed.* The jury is the last check against tyranny! We walked out free people!

The main government investigator, "Bob," being very experienced, some days before the verdicts were delivered, saw what was happening. He was not there to hear the verdicts. He said to me after my witnesses had taken the stand and after I had testified, "Mr. Crenshaw, you don't have anything to worry about." The lead prosecutor was in the hospital with ulcerative colitis. (Did she hate us that badly?) If we won everything, I really wanted both of them there, but I might have gloated. As it was, all the glory went to the Triune God, as it should have. There was only the young backup prosecutor there that day, and at the last verdict he exited another door so he would not have to confront us. The judge herself left quickly. We walked out, free people, out the door where the court guards and other guards were, who were smiling and shaking our hands vigorously. Over the months, they had come to like and respect us.

I grabbed my co-defendants and said that we must give God the glory so we went to an empty room down the hall. I stood on a chair and read Psalm 2, the whole Psalm, but here is part of it:

> Why do the nations rage,
> And the people plot a vain thing?
> The kings of the earth set themselves,
> And the rulers take counsel together,
> Against the LORD and against His [Messiah],

*saying*, "Let us break Their bonds in pieces
And cast away Their cords from us."
He who sits in the heavens shall laugh;
The Lord shall hold them in derision. (Psalm 2:1-4)

Franklin Sanders then took my Bible and read another Psalm, and then another. There were praises in prayer. We walked out free people to the glory of the Lion of the Tribe of Judah, and as C. S. Lewis said, "He is not a tame Lion."

I called Ruth at home from court, and she answered with great concern in her voice.

I said, "We have verdicts. Are you ready for this?" I heard her take a deep breath.

"All defendants on all counts, NOT GUILTY." She began to cry, laugh, squeal, and rejoice all together. After 18 months, the joy and release were huge. She called everyone we knew, and when I got home, there was no one for me to call. She almost broke my neck with hugs and kisses when I arrived home. Our children were jumping up and down and running through the house.

## Our Celebrations

Then it would seem that God has a sense of humor. We were arrested on January 9th, 1990 and acquitted on July 9th, 1991, exactly three periods to the day of six months, 6-6-6. **Talk about timing!**

As the verdicts were being read, the attorney to my right said to me, "This is going to cost me a bundle." I could not imagine what he meant, as the government had paid him $40 an hour for preparation time outside court and $60 an hour for in court time. Ninety-nine percent of the time, he just sat there, read books, or doodled. Then he reminded me that he had promised that he would pay for a party in down town Memphis at a swanky restaurant, *if* we won every count. No one thought that possible so it was soon forgotten; we won all counts on the last day of the trial, as the Lord Christ revealed His trump suit, and the attorney paid up!

Right after the verdicts, one of the lead attorneys, not a Christian but who became one later, said to me,

"We really kicked their butts, didn't we?"

Cold chills went down my spine. We must not be arrogant or cocky about that victory; it was not **ours**, it was **His**. Every human means we used seem to accomplish nothing, but it was my short-sightedness that did not see His hand in the details from the beginning. But if we all had gone to jail, that would have been His grace as well. He is in charge and does what is best for His people.

We often hear that the "devil is in the details." In this case, King Jesus was in the details, from the arrests to the choosing of the jury to the timing of appeals court decisions to the demeanor of the pint-sized, squeaky voice, female prosecutor to the bias of the judge against us. The jury saw through it all.

We found out after the trial that the first eleven jurors were for us, number twelve was not, but she had to leave for her daughter's surgery, and then juror thirteen was for us. How did that happen? The Lord of glory stacked the deck.

Once the trial was over, the jury told us that besides the lack of substantial evidence against us, the collusion between the prosecution and the judge was another reason they acquitted us, which collusion was communicated by facial expressions of the judge to the prosecution, the jury said. I mentioned earlier that the judge was always saying for us to maintain a neutral face in the presence of the jury, but they noticed the judge's antics. After the trial, the jury said,

"The judge must think we are stupid if she thinks she can make all those faces to influence us."

Moreover, we had prayed the Monday night the jury received the trial that if a juror were holding out, he/she would come around the next morning, and later we discovered that was exactly what happened!

We had a party the night of the verdicts (Tuesday), then Wednesday night, Thursday night, Friday night, and Saturday night. We had two worship services on Sunday to accommodate so many people, attorneys with their wives or husbands, others who had supported us, with the Rev. Dan Morse preaching one service and yours truly the other one. We reveled in grace.

## That Great and Terrible Last Day

As good as those verdicts were, they pale into insignificance compared to being delivered from the wrath of God at the Last Day judgment. As we gather in the Lord's presence on that dreadful day, we Christians shall be openly acknowledged and acquitted.

The books will be opened with the record of our sins. All those who wanted justice will now receive it. There is no higher court than this one, and everyone will be judged by His sovereign majesty, the King of all the ages, whose Name is above every name. He is the prosecuting attorney who has never lost.

Since He is *omnipresent,* He is the eye-witness to all our sins that we have committed in thought, word, or deed.

Since He is *omniscient,* He knows all our sins, even of the heart.

Since He is *perfect justice,* He is the Judge and jury.

Since He is *omnipotent,* He is the executioner.

The great irony is that at our earthly trial, we all confessed that we were not guilty, and we were found such. But at this trial at the

Last Day, the only ones who escape everlasting punishment (Matt. 25:46) are those who have confessed they are guilty and claimed the blood of the substitute, the Lamb of God, but we must confess Him now, before we die. After death, it is too late (Heb. 9:27).

We shall celebrate around the great throne, never to be separated again, and so shall we ever be with the Lord to sing the song of the Lamb:

> "Blessing and honor and glory and power be to Him who sits on the throne, and to the Lamb, forever and ever!" (Rev. 5:13)

**But this book you are reading is about God's timing**. For 18 months we worked on copying records (we spent weeks doing so at our expense so we could prepare for the trial), worked on trial details (I prepared my own witnesses and the questions we would ask), and for all those months, nothing seemed to be going our way. Once in disgust I said at a court break, "When are we ever going to win anything." Dan Morse said, "At the verdicts." **The Lord waited until the last possible minute, the last day of the trial, and He was right on time!** We were completely exonerated! How sweet it was!

# Chapter 15: IRS Audit

Since the IRS and the government failed to convict us criminally, they audited us civilly—every defendant. In late 1992, I received my audit letter. One cannot receive a court appointed attorney for civil matters, and I did not have the money to hire one for six years back tax returns. What was I going to do?

While I was praying over that matter, one day I went to the bank for my grandparents. As I got out of the car, there was a friend whom I had known casually from the past. I did not see him, but he said something to me. Jim had followed our case in the news, and was very interested in how we were exonerated. I gave him a brief synopsis, and then I casually said that I had received an IRS audit letter. Jim said:

"Do you have someone to represent you for that audit? It is rare for them to go back six years unless they expect something, and in your case—and the case of all the defendants—obviously they want to continue the trial. You definitely don't want to go this alone. If you don't have anyone, I would be glad to do so."

Then I recalled that not only was Jim a fine attorney, he specialized in the IRS tax code. I also recalled that he did not like to lose at anything, especially in his field of expertise. He had been Richard's attorney on retainer at the carpet company. I eagerly said I would be grateful for his help, but that I had little money to pay.

"What will you charge?"

"Let's don't worry about that now. Can you bring the IRS letter to me, and let's see what they want? We'll assess it, and plan from there. I'll go to the audit, and you stay home."

I was glad to hear him say stay home as at that point in my life, I did not want to see them or breathe the same air.

Jim and I met many times, and I did much research to validate my income and deductions. Each time we met I asked Jim what I owed him, that I needed to pay along as I could not give him a lump sum at the end. He would always say, "Let's not worry about that right now." The auditor was very tough, not allowing me anything. When Jim found out that she was the wife of one of the criminal in-vestigators of our case, he was livid.

"This is a huge conflict of interest for you to be auditing a man who was the focus of your husband's investigation. You should have recused yourself; not to do so is illegal. You take your best shot at my client; I'm going straight to appeals."

She allowed us nothing; appeals allowed us everything. Jim came to me with an agreement, and said I should sign it. I did, and I only owed a reasonable amount so I signed it.

At our last meeting, when I signed the agreement, I asked Jim one more time what I owed. He held out his hand, and said: "Have a nice life." I owed the IRS a considerable amount, at least for me, but did not have the money. It was the Fall of 1993.

If you recall from the end of chapter ten, in the Fall of 1993 VA sent me an offer to pay them off and get back in their graces. The payoff was 40% off. The IRS offered me a deal on appeal that was about 80% off from what the original auditor wanted. Now I had two large debts that I could settle at a percentage of what they could have been, both having come due in the Fall of 1993, but no money. What was I do? The Lord had that covered also, for my paternal grandmother had passed away some months before, and just at that time, the Fall of 1993, I received a small inheritance. **Talk about tim-**

**ing! I paid off both VA and the IRS the same month!** I never took bankruptcy.

Once again the Lord's timing was excellent. I just "happened" to bump into Jim at the bank, the result of the audit was God's grace, and Jim had done all his work free of charge. It just "happened" that VA offered me a payoff. It just "happened" that the IRS offered me a payoff. It just "happened" that my inheritance came through at the same time. **Of course, the Lord let the VA and IRS debts pile up first to make me sweat before he blessed me with the inheritance.** Truly, God is good, but the government had put me through a lot.

Do I hate the USA? Absolutely not; it is still one of the greatest nations in the history of mankind. I pray every Sunday, and sometimes during the week, for spiritual revival in our beloved nation. Revival does not begin with the government, but with the Church, and more particularly with me, personally. Yet I admit that I've become cynical regarding our laws and politics. When Barak Obama can receive the Nobel Peace Prize even before doing anything, what is there left for cynicism? But my hope is in Christ, in the Church that has rejected its own standards, and that it would repent and return to those standards. (Get my book on the Ten Commandments, titled *NOT Ten Suggestions* (www.ftstl.com.). There is hope but only in Christ; let us look to Him (2 Chron. 7:14).

> If My people who are called by My name will humble themselves, and pray and seek My face, and <u>turn from their wicked ways</u>, **then** I will hear from heaven, and will forgive their sin and heal their land.

# Chapter 16: Earning a Doctorate

## Mindless Research

After I was received into the Reformed Episcopal Church in May 1991, I found myself very involved in ministry, such as liturgy, preaching, teaching, being with my people, counseling, visiting, baptisms, marriages, and more. Once when I was on vacation with Ruth and our two kids, I kept seeing books written by word of faith authors. While she drove, I read. At that time (1991), virtually no one had researched them. I researched every aspect of them, and was thinking of writing something up. Someone suggested that I submit it as a doctoral thesis if I could get it approved. I pursued that. Later it would become a book with foreword by John MacArthur and endorsement by Michael Scott Horton, and the title is *Man as God: The Word of Faith Movement* (available from Barnes and Noble web site or www.ftstl.com).

Meanwhile, our diocese was starting a seminary in Shreveport, LA, Cranmer Theological House, and Bp. Grote asked me to teach the biblical languages. It would help if I had a doctorate. I began teaching Greek in September 1994, and I received the Th. D. in October 1994! **God was one month "late"!** When I began the research, a Th. D. was not in my thoughts at all. **Who can figure God's timing?**

I drove to Shreveport from Memphis twice a month from 1994 to 1996, and the first year I taught Greek and the second year Hebrew. Then in 1996, Bp. Grote asked me to move to Amarillo, TX to work in a church there for two years. There was a good man there who had graduated from another seminary but needed to be helped along with a view to taking the church. The idea was that I would work there for two years, continue to drive to Shreveport to teach Greek and Hebrew, and then Bp. Grote would move me to Shreveport to be full time with Cranmer House in 1998. I agreed to that. Thus, I became the Academic Dean in 1998 and the dean in 2004.

## Problems in Shreveport

In February 2001, Ruth and I drove from Shreveport to Corpus Christi for our annual diocesan meeting, and we had to negotiate Houston traffic. I turned to Ruth and said, "I'm never moving to Houston." Guess where I was in July?

In 2001 problems arose with the Shreveport location for the seminary, and we decided to relocate in Houston. I have notes on what happened to force the move, but it would not be profitable to give the details. Ruth and I had to put our house on the market, and within 24 hours we had three contracts! **Talk about timing!**

Bp. Grote had promised another professor and me two years salary if we moved to Houston with the seminary, but he was able to get us three years, from 2001 to 2004. Then in early 2004 we were running out of money, and the other professor got a job in another seminary. For me two things came together, once again out of the blue. I began a Lay Institute program, and several others and I began St. Francis Anglican Church, both in January 2004. Unknown to me at first, a layman had been giving money to the diocese to form a church in the area where I live (!), which was the seed money. The Lay Institute quickly grew into full time students for the seminary, and we began St. Francis in my living room as a Bible study. **Once again, just as I was on the edge, the Lord's timing was at the last minute, but right on time**. Today I'm supported mostly as pastor of St. Francis Church but also as Dean of Cranmer Theological House.

# Chapter 17: Colon Cancer?

## Routine Colonoscopy

I had a routine colonoscopy in 2004 at the VA hospital. They gave me a muscle relaxer which did nothing for the pain, and I was fully conscious during the procedure.

"Doc, whatever you gave me, it is not working."

He said to the nurse, "Give him a little more of the muscle relaxer."

Still, it did nothing. He said, "Now roll on your right side." Then after a couple of minutes, "Roll on your left side." I kept hearing someone moan, and realized it was me.

It was excruciating. After it was over, he told me he found a polyp, but thought it was benign. He would have it analyzed. I heard nothing, and VA forgot to have a follow up exam two years later.

Six years later it dawned on me that I needed another colonoscopy, so I decided to go a civilian doctor. I wanted to be unconscious this time, so I made arrangements. It was September 2010, and I knew nothing but sweet dreams. My wife told me later that the doctor had found a polyp the size of a lemon, that it was too large for him to remove, and that it would have to be surgically removed. He recommended a surgeon.

I went to the surgeon and had him look over the test results. He agreed that it would have to come out. I said, "What happens if we do nothing?"

He said, "Oh, you'll get cancer."

I responded, "When do we go to surgery?"

A time was set only a couple of weeks out. I was put into a deep sleep, he went in through my naval, and took out 14 inches of my colon. I was in the hospital about five days. The most miserable aspect of the surgery was not the pain after surgery but that horrible tube down my throat. After several days of struggling with it, a nurse said it was not down far enough as nothing was being pumped up. So she took it out, and put another tube through my nose, her hand shaking as she pushed hard to make it go through the membrane. I bled like a stuck hog, but finally it was placed.

Each day the surgeon would come in to see how I was doing, and each time I pleaded to get that tube out. He said, "You must pass gas, and then we can remove it."

"What? You mean I have to fart?"

"That's right?"

"Why?"

"That way we know that your colon is connecting to your intestine correctly."

A couple of days later, just as he was coming in my room, I let out a loud one. He bellowed, "Take that tube out!" What a relief! My throat felt like someone had sandpapered it then poured alcohol down it, but at least the tube was out.

I stayed home for a week or longer, and made an appointment to see the surgeon again. Once Ruth and I were in his office, he went over what he had done. Finally, I asked him if it was cancerous, and he said, "Yes, but I got it all."

Ruth almost lost it. He explained that he took out enough colon to make sure it was all gone. Ruth said something like, "If the cancer is still there, what might happen . . ." and he interrupted, "No, I did not say *if* I got all of it but that I . . GOT . . IT . . ALL," pausing between the words for emphasis. Then we had to schedule a visit to the kind of doctor I never wanted to see—an oncologist, a cancer doctor. Ruth and I were not sure how to interpret going to an oncologist if the surgeon got it all. Did that mean there could be cancer cells in the blood even if he removed the "lemon"?

## Going to the Oncologist

We had another two weeks or so to wait to see the oncologist. The surgeon said that he had taken a large amount of lymph node samples and sent them out to be analyzed, and I took those records to the oncologist, who had also ordered blood work before I saw him.

We were in the patient room, and after some time, he entered, introduced himself, and said he needed to see the lymph node results and the blood work he had ordered.

He took a *long* time, analyzed the reports carefully, drew all kinds of diagrams and pictures on large paper, and did not say a word. I tried to analyze his face, but it was neutral. I felt like I was waiting for another verdict, and in a sense I was. Ruth and I held our breath. After about 30 minutes, he looked at us with a large smile and said,

"I don't see signs of cancer anywhere, not in your lymph nodes or in your blood. Congratulations, you're cancer free, and you don't need chemo or radiation. But the cells from the 'lemon' the surgeon removed were indeed well on their way to being cancerous. A little longer, and you would have had a serious case of cancer."

Then he showed us how cells change and what stage the cells were in on their way to cancer, which was most of the way there. I've had about seven follow up exams with him complete with blood work, and the results have all been the same. **Talk about timing!**

**God came through at the last minute, but He was right on time!**

Praise the Lord!

# Chapter 18: Suddenly Home

Ruth and I went to Knoxville where my Uncle Jim lives to celebrate our 42$^{nd}$ anniversary, July, 2011. We spent the night just outside Gatlinburg, TN, where we had taken our kids many times on vacations. (Now they are taking their kids on vacations.) I was in Gatlinburg in a leather shop looking at belts, and Ruth was standing at the doorway with the traffic behind her. She has hearing aids. Her cell phone rang, and our son was on the line.

"Momma, where are you? I hear traffic."

"We're walking Gatlinburg, Trace, what do you want, sweetheart?"

"I have bad news, momma."

"What? I can't hear you?"

"I have bad news."

"You have bad what? Here, talk to daddy."

"Hello, Trace, is that you? There is a lot of noise, and we're only a few feet from the street."

"I have bad news, daddy. Dylan's mother has been killed in a car wreck."

"Who? Did you say Ms. Janet?"

"Yes."

"Dylan's mother?"

"Yes."

"Are you sure there has not been a mistake?"

"I don't think so. The Highway Patrol has talked to Jerry, her husband."

"Horrible. I'll call Dylan."

"Dylan, this is your father-in-law. Is what I heard about your mother true?"

"I guess it is. I'm still trying to take it in."

"I'm so sorry. We'll cut short our vacation and will see you tomorrow. We'll help out as soon as we get there, and we'll be praying for you and the family all the way back to Memphis."

"We're really going to need it. Thank you."

Those two, one minute conversations changed our lives forever. Our daughter, Chandra (pronounced "SHAWN-drah"), met Dylan in our youth group at Immanuel Reformed Episcopal Church, and they never dated anyone but one another. My good friend since 1984, Bp. Morse, who was also their pastor, was scheduled to perform the wedding, but he had a bad wreck the month before the wedding. Bp. Grote graciously performed it in May 1999.

Janet Smith, Dylan's mother, was one the most gracious people I've ever met. Indeed, *she never met a person she did not love to serve.* There were never any in-law problems, either on her side or ours. She loved our daughter from the beginning, and we loved Dylan. She was easy to love, for she was self-giving and accepted people the way they were.

When I tell people how close we all were (are), in-laws and all, they look at me with a blank stare. They don't see how I, as Dylan's father-in-law, would care that much if his mother died. But the gospel in a family binds us together so that we are all close. When one member hurts, we all hurt.

When Bp. Morse gave Dylan and Chandra permission to marry, we were all delighted. Once the marriage had become reality, Janet often invited us to her house, and her other son, Jacob, was often there. At Christmas she included Ruth and me as part of the family, and we all exchanged gifts.

Dylan's parents, like mine, had divorced when he was much younger. I never asked the reason. Sometime after Dylan and Chandra were married, Janet began to date Jerry, and they discovered that he had a brain tumor. Most women would have said goodbye, but she married him so she could take better care of him! Incredible, especially in this selfish age. She was a top RN, as evidenced by all the co-workers who attended her funeral, standing room only. She knew how to do things regarding the care of her husband that most would not. It was not that she was marrying money, for Jerry was a mail carrier, not a rich tycoon, but also a Christian man. She married him for love and commitment, rare qualities in our godless society. Janet and Jerry often had Ruth and me, along with our son and his wife and children, to their lakeside home in the country outside Memphis. Of course, Dylan and Chandra would be there, and we all had good times together.

Janet was very supportive of her two sons, Dylan and Jacob, and would often be there to help them financially if they needed it. Chandra loved Ms. Janet, like a mother, and her own mother, Ruth, supported that. So did I.

Janet had been working out details to help her father get home from the hospital, and as an RN she would see that things went smoothly. He had a serious condition and was not expected to live much longer. She was on the expressway at Memphis driving to the hospital, and a wreck had stopped traffic. She stopped; the person behind her did not. Suddenly, she was home with the Lord, leaving her husband, whose tumor she had helped to nurse until it had no signs of being there; and leaving two sons, both married, but only

Dylan with kids. She would never see the grandkids she loved so much grow up, or would she? We don't really know. Jacob and his wife, Carrie, now have a son, and Janet does not know it, or does she? Perhaps she does.

I baptized Dylan's and Chandra's first child, a boy named Donovan, and then I had just recently baptized the second one, a girl, Elayna. She was the first girl on Dylan's side for several generations, and Janet was looking forward to spoiling her. We did not know if she would make it to the baptism or not because of her job, but she did, and brought a new christening dress for her granddaughter. No one was surprised she did that.

Janet's father died within 36 hours of her being killed on the expressway so we had a double funeral, daughter and father, together. A Methodist minister took care of the details of the funeral, read the scriptures, and prayed, and I preached the message. It makes it much easier when the deceased are believers in Jesus. They both were.

**But what about the timing of these deaths?** One was expected to die, being on in years; no one thought Janet would die, who was in her mid-50s. Everyone would have thought that surely her father, and perhaps her husband with the tumor, would have died first. Why would God allow such an event, or is it too strong to say He *planned* such an event? The mystery of God's sovereignty is that we use our wills and plan, but somehow God Almighty is also involved. Janet was needed by her husband, by her dad and mom, by all those she helped as an RN, by her children, and her grandchildren. This little book is about God's gracious timing in His providence in our lives. If there was ever an event in my life where it seems that God blew it, this would seem to qualify. **"Bad timing, Lord, bad timing, indeed."** How do we respond?

One reason things seem wrong is that we do not have the whole picture. Perhaps later we can see something of what He was doing. When I was a small boy, my grandmother Shussie would hook rugs. She had a large wooden frame easel, and she would devise the colors, pictures, and hook the appropriate thread into the developing rug. One night I was playing on the floor, and looked up. It looked awful, random, with no pattern, strings hanging down.

I said, "Shussie, what are you making. It looks like nothing but strings."

She said, "Get up, and see it from the top."

When I saw it from her view, it was beautiful, well designed and patterned. That is the way our lives look to God. We see things from the "bottom," but He sees things from the "top," from His view, and the design and pattern are beautiful.

Here is perhaps another reason for her death. This past Christmas when Ruth and I were home in Memphis, we all met at my son's house. He led us in a time of thanksgiving, that each person would gives thanks for one thing in their lives. When it came Chandra's time, she said, with tears,

"I thank God that Ms. Janet's death has led to my husband being in hyper-spiritual growth mode."

It was a painful statement, and yet very insightful statement, full of love and trust in Christ without knowing all the reasons. **The timing of her death was painful**, but the Lord of the Church knows what He is doing. We rest in that.

Consider a time when Jesus was "late" and someone died because of it. There was a man named Lazarus, the sister of the Mary who had anointed Jesus' feet, and Lazarus was very sick. Mary was full of angst, and sent word to Jesus to come heal him:

> Therefore the sisters sent to Him, saying, "Lord, behold, he whom You love is sick." When Jesus heard *that*, He said, "This sickness is not unto death, but for the glory of God, that the Son of God may be glorified through it." **Now Jesus loved Martha and her sister and Lazarus. So, when He heard that he was sick, He stayed two more days in the place where He was** (John 11:3-6).

Notice the words in bold print: Jesus loved Mary and Lazarus. Then notice the next word: "So," which draws a conclusion. In other words, **because** Jesus loved Lazarus, He let him die! Time was of the essence, but apparently Jesus did not care enough to get there quickly. **Talk about bad timing!** Haven't we all thought that Jesus was late or that He didn't really care? If He did care, why doesn't He relieve this trial now, not tomorrow? The reason may be "for the glory of God," and when the deliverance comes, it will be sweeter. Mary indirectly rebuked the Lord when He finally came:

> "Lord, if you had been here, my brother would not have died" (John 11:32).

Mary had several misconceptions about Jesus that only these circumstances could cure. First, she thought Jesus had not been there when her brother had died. As God in the flesh, which she had only minutes before confessed, He *was* there.

Second, she thought that death was the trump card, even over Jesus, and that there was a master that even Jesus must bow to.

When Jesus had just proclaimed that He was the resurrection and the life, she had responded:

> "Yes, Lord, I believe that You are the Christ, the Son of God, who is to come into the world" (John 11:27).

She just didn't get the majesty of His person, nor would we have done any better, nor do we in our lives do much better now. We have the full revelation of who Christ is—and I teach that course in seminary—but I have to be reminded, practically, of that truth, like Mary and those around her.

So the eternal I AM asks where Lazarus is laid, saying again that the sickness was for the glory of God. Here is what He did and said:

> Jesus said, "Take away the stone." Martha, the sister of him who was dead, said to Him, "**Lord, by this time there is a stench, for he has been dead four days.**" Jesus said to her, "Did I not say to you that if you would believe you would see the glory of God?" Then they took away the stone *from the place* where the dead man was lying. And Jesus lifted up *His* eyes and said, "Father, I thank You that You have heard Me. And I know that You always hear Me, but because of the people who are standing by I said *this*, that they may believe that You sent Me." Now when He had said these things, He cried with a loud voice, "**Lazarus, come forth**!" And he who had died **came out** bound hand and foot with grave clothes, and his face was wrapped with a cloth. Jesus said to them, "Loose him, and let him go" (John 11:39-44).

Did Lazarus die and could Jesus not do anything about it? No, *Jesus was in control of the circumstances from the time that He delayed two more days.* Then why did Lazarus die when he did? It was for the glory of God and for the growth in faith of those around him. Was Lazarus an unwilling pawn on Jesus' chess board, brought to life only to die again later? No! Jesus loved Lazarus and only did that which was good for both him and his sisters and friends. We can never probe the mystery of God's sovereignty so just enjoy it, and don't try to figure it out.

Thus, a third take on Janet's death is that we Christians take death too seriously. It is not the end but the beginning. For the Christian, it is like walking from one house to another, from one place to live to the final place. Death for the Christian is not final, it is initial, the beginning of life indeed. We may be separated from Janet for 50 years, but contrast that with being with her forever. Who was it who said, "It ain't over till it's over"? For the Christian, it "ain't" ever over, for he/she is brought into the presence of the crucified, dead, and resurrected One. (It's not over for the non-Christian either, but this book is not about hell.) For the Christian, it is "absent from the body, present with the Lord" (2 Cor. 5:8).

Also, though death is an enemy, we have been delivered from it:

> Inasmuch then as the children have partaken of flesh and blood, He Himself likewise shared in the same, that through death He might destroy him who had the power of death, that is, the devil, and **release those who through fear of death were all their lifetime subject to bondage** (Heb. 2:14-15).

We win, Satan loses. We grieve, but not as those who have no hope (1 Thess. 4:13). Biblical hope is not a maybe but a certainty. Christians die into reality, not out of reality, into hope, not out of hope. Death for us is not despair, the end, but it is hope, the beginning. We transition from trials into peace. We do not die into nothingness but into His presence where nothing will ever be able to harm us again.

The death of Janet on one level was a tragedy, and we all miss her, especially at Christmas time. Did she die "before [her] time," as Ecclesiastes 7:17 says? No, Ecclesiastes is referring to those who give themselves over to wickedness and so self-destruct, not living out a full life. It was her time, and it was our time to learn to trust. Those who depended on her would now have to depend solely on Jesus.

At the end of Ms. Janet's funeral in my sermon I related this story from C. S. Lewis, the former agnostic of England. Jack (as Lewis was called by his friends) was walking with a friend in 1963. Jack crossed the street, and his friend yelled,

"Goodbye Jack."

When Jack got to the other side and the traffic cleared, he turned and yelled back,

"Christians never say **goodbye** to Christians; they say '**See you later**.'"

Dylan and Jacob, your mother is waiting for you.

# Chapter 19: Summing It Up

I have lived a charmed life, and I don't mean magic charms, but by the sovereign grace of the King of kings. I do not know what the future holds, but I know the One who holds the future. It has not been my alleged superior faith or supposed merit that has worked such incredible timing throughout my whole life.

I've found that most of our trials and problems are from lack of contentment. The Puritan Jeremiah Burroughs wrote *The Rare Jewel of Christian Contentment*, which I read many years ago. It is very convicting but a gem. As one man stated, "Contentment is as rare among men as it is natural among animals, and no form of government has ever satisfied its subjects" (Will Durant, *Caesar and Christ*, 1971, p. 22).

So what makes something to be a trial? Is it not that we don't like it? If we liked it, it would, by definition, not be a trial. The more the Triune God lavishes gifts on us, the more we expect Him to do so; and if we are without for a season, we become angry at Him and want Him to take us back to our "normal" state of affairs.

Take a person, any person, give him $500 on Monday, then $500 on the next Monday, and so on for three months. Then skip two weeks, and will he not be angry that you skipped those two weeks? What began as grace now has become duty. So we do with God. He has lavished material prosperity and many blessings on us in the USA even beyond what the Pharaohs of old had, more than any nation in history. He gives us good health, keeps our friends and relatives alive, but let one thing be taken away, and we're ready to take Job's wife's advice: "Curse God and die" (Job 2:9). God cares about our souls (and

of course our bodies and meeting our physical needs), about our being conformed to the moral image of His Son. We care about the
abundance of things we possess (Luke 12:15), watching TV, the nice
cars that others will admire, pilling up toys to leave to someone who
has not worked to attain them, and who will probably squander
them. There is a bumper sticker that says, "He who dies with the most
toys wins." But consider what God says through His servant, the
Apostle Paul:

> Therefore we do not lose heart. Even though our
> outward man is perishing, yet the inward *man* is being
> renewed day by day. For our light affliction, which is but
> for a moment, is working for us a far more exceeding
> *and* eternal weight of glory, while we do not look at the
> things which are seen, but at the things which are not
> seen. For the things which are seen are temporal, but
> the things which are not seen are eternal (2 Cor. 4:15-
> 18).

Notice the contrasts:
- Outward man vs. inward man
- Light affliction, for just a moment vs. weight of glory for-
  ever
- Things seen vs. things not seen
- Temporal vs. eternal

It is trials that drive us to use the means of grace, for while we
are prosperous we think we have no need, for we are then self-suffi-
cient, we think. It is trials that drive us to the mercy seat for grace:

> For we do not have a High Priest who cannot sym-
> pathize with our weaknesses, but was in all *points*
> tempted as *we are, yet* without sin. Let us therefore

come boldly to the throne of grace, **that we may ob-
tain mercy and find grace to help in time of need**
(Heb. 4:15-16).

Recall the mythical Greek god Antaeus, son of his earth goddess
mother. When Hercules wrestled the giant, he would throw him to
the earth. When Antaeus made contact with his earth goddess mother, she would renew his strength to fight Hercules again. When Hercules realized how his strength was returning, he picked up Antaeus
off the ground and crushed him in his arms. We are like Antaeus, but
we serve no mythical God. When we are knocked down, we fall on
Christ, we go to Him in prayer, we read our Bibles, we attend worship,
and we are renewed, only better than Antaeus. Satan is Hercules, but
he cannot crush us, for the Sovereign King has promised that the
gates of hell will not prevail against us (Matt. 16:18). In Christ, we are
invincible.

We don't know how to depend on God so He teaches us by re-
moving human crutches such as jobs, money, loved ones who supply
our financial needs, and then we *have* to depend on Him. It is scary
when that happens, for we have lost control, as if we ever had it. Our
continued success in the USA and in our Christian lives will weaken
the sense of dependence on providence (R. L. Dabney, *Our Secular
Poverty*); and if we gain much money, we buy more toys. The Lord
said that the one who uses his money for His kingdom will keep it
(rewards in heaven), but the one who hoards it will lose it (judgment,
Matt. 10:39).

Do I have any regrets? The one who doesn't is either perfect or
an arrogant fool. I have tried to learn from the past, though I sometimes repeat the same sins. The only people who do not change are

in cemeteries. All I want from this life is one statement: "Well done thou good and faithful servant" (Matt. 25:21).

I've left out some of **God's timings in my life**, and I'm sure there are others I'm not aware of. But here is what we've seen:

- A wreck saved my mother's life, **just in time**. (1958)
- Many times in Vietnam I was spared, not only from accidents with grenades and plastic charges, but also from incoming mortar rounds and rockets. I was on the last Chinook out of a terrible situation, the last aircraft out, one of the last three on the Chinook, **just in time**. (1968)
- I only received one injury in Vietnam, in my right forearm, which permanently removed an idol, bowling.
- The two years in the Army took away any desire to redirect my life toward pipe dreams and forced me to be disciplined. My grades went from F's to A's. God removed not only the bowling but also the engineering to direct me to the ministry. I went from electrical engineering to the Army to Bible College to seminary. Some got to seminary quicker, but Jesus had to take me the long way, which was my fault. **His timing**, coupled with His patience, got me there.
- Just before I graduated from Mid-South Bible College, a non-accredited school, it became accredited, and I was accepted to Dallas Theological Seminary, an accredited seminary. I was the first student from MSBC to go there, and got accepted **just in time for the academic year of 1972**. Thus, my Th. M. degree was accredited.
- The microfilming job at the Savings and Loan when I entered seminary coincided exactly with how long it took me to grad-

uate: from July 1972 to May 1976. Ruth got her job at the same place in 24 hours of when we first went to Dallas to look for her a job in May 1972. **How is that for timing?**

- After seminary, I worked one summer translating Hebrew, in Wilmington, DE, rented my house to Christian friends who needed the house *just for that summer,* **perfect timing**. (1976)

- When I was returning from Wilmington, DE back to Dallas, without a job, I stopped in Memphis, talked to my new friend I had met as I had gone through Memphis to Wilmington. He asked me to candidate for his church. I did, and continued to Dallas with a job, put our house on the market to sell, and moved to Memphis area to pastor my first church. After a year, I resigned so I could determine where my theology was going.

- **At that precise moment** (!), a friend had been made head master of a Christian school so he hired me to teach there. The school did not continue financially, so I was hired at another Christian school. Likewise, at the end of the year, it also failed financially. Just as I was about to be hired at a very stable Christian school (still going strong), a "friend" violated my confidence and grabbed the teaching job behind my back. (1979)

- Just as I was running out of money, another friend came to town to look at the possibility of starting a Christian book store, and asked me if I knew anyone who would like to manage it. I said, "Yes, me," and I got the job, **just in time to make bills**. (1979)

- That job lasted 1 ½ years, and due to flooding in Memphis, the bridge where many people came to the store was washed out, and though the store could be reached by a longer route, it still hurt sales. I was fired, then given back the job, but left it to work in an insurance and investment company that Christian business men recommended.
- Now it is 1981. At the insurance company, I discovered a fraud scheme and lost that job, was working in one Presbyterian church with a view to becoming pastor, but was turned down, and conducted a church trial at another Presbyterian church. I was dead broke, my wife was driving an 80 mile paper route, and I was putting out brochures for my friend's carpet company. **God's timing seemed off this time, for sure, but . . .**
- In 1982 with my grandmother's help, I became my friend's business partner in his floor covering company.
- In 1986, I resigned from the Presbyterian Church in Atoka, TN, and became the associate pastor at the church I had helped to start.
- In 1987, my good friend Richard moved to Arkansas to be with his parents, began a new floor covering company, offered me the one in Memphis free, but the **timing was good for me to go back into the ministry full time**. I had some good years until 1990.
- From January 9th, 1990 to July 9th, 1991, I was arrested, tried, and found innocent. **There were key points of timing** in the big federal trial, such as Supreme Court case and an Appeals court decision that gave us more freedom to present our case in court. We lost everything in court, just about, until the last

day (what a prefigure for at the ultimate Last Day, the elect shall be openly acknowledged and acquitted!). On the very last day of the trial, when the verdicts were read, we won all 46 counts. Defendants, 46; government, 0. **That was God's perfect timing!**

- Then I earned a doctorate, not having a clue why I was doing it. One generally needs that to teach in seminary, but I had given up on that dream 20 years ago. After I submitted the thesis, I began teaching at Cranmer Theological House in September 1994, and the Th.D. was awarded in October 1994. **How is that for timing?**

- The seminary was in Shreveport, LA, but we hit a snag and had to move to Houston. After three years (early 2004), we were out of money, within several months of closing the seminary, but the Lord gave us a Lay Institute program, that gave us full-time students who paid tuition, and I and others began St. Francis REC in my home in January 2004. Now the church primarily and the seminary secondarily pay my salary.

What is ahead? I'm now 67 (February 2012), and I don't know. I would like to retire, at least mostly, to research and write, but that is in His hands. When Ruth and I began dating, our theme verse was Matthew 6:33, already mentioned in this book:

> "Seek ye first the kingdom of God and His righteousness, and all these things will be added to you."

I hope I've made it clear that I strongly believe in using human means to make things happen. In fact, I can get on the nerves of those around me when things need "fixing," for I usually become very intense to work things out. I work as if everything depended on me.

Then I try to obey the Lord's written Word, and finally I trust His providence as if everything depends on Him, because it does.

I put little trust in riches, though I believe in storing up as much as possible, like the ant (Prov. 6:6ff), but when all has been done, it is the Lord who prospers or who does not prosper. I've seen professing Christians chase get rich-quick-schemes (like me!), such as the real estate bubble, or pyramid schemes, or they convince themselves it is not a get rich quick scheme, only a temporary pursuit. They convince themselves that they will quit soon. Just a little more money; it becomes an addiction, the worship of another god: "covetousness is idolatry" (Col. 3:5). They sacrifice their children, lose time with them that can never be recovered, send them to public schools to get educated where God's morality is denied because they allegedly can't afford it (a few really can't), while many of them drive nice cars and live in nice homes, which is not wrong, unless other priorities are sacrificed, and then their children leave the church for the world. They wonder what happened. They think their security is the accumulation of assets rather than in the Lord and His promises.

Several years ago someone I know was approached by a company that said he could earn $250,000 in a couple of years with a little sacrifice. He asked what was meant by sacrifice. The employer said,

"You might have to give up some weekends and work longer days for a while."

He responded, "I go to church on Sundays, and spend the weekends and most nights with my children, not to mention my wife. How will I ever recapture that lost time with them?"

There is someone who has his priorities right. Time is like water, once poured out, it can never be regained, never. It is gone forever. God gives us all the same amount of time; we're all on an equal playing field. So what is really important? Is it retirement accounts or the true riches (Luke 16:11)? We can easily lose earthly treasures, but the heavenly treasures cannot be lost:

> Blessed be the God and Father of our Lord Jesus Christ, who according to His abundant mercy has begotten us again to a living hope through the resurrection of Jesus Christ from the dead, to an **inheritance incorruptible** and **undefiled** and that **does not fade away, reserved** in heaven for you, who are kept by the power of God through faith for salvation ready to be revealed in the last time (1 Peter 1:3-5).

Moths cannot destroy it, and thieves cannot steal it. What shall we give our children, money or the faith? Of course, both would be nice, but we must emphasize the Christian faith. As one gospel song used to put it, modern parents too often say, "Not I love you, honey, but here take some money." We have reared a generation of "Christians" who love money and who don't have a clue how to live life. They allow their children to marry non-Christians. My exhortation is walk in faith, walk boldly, God's promises are faithful. I've tested them and not found them wanting.

> Remember my affliction and roaming, the wormwood and the gall. My soul still remembers and sinks within me. This I recall to my mind, therefore I have hope. Through the LORD'S mercies we are not consumed, because His compassions fail not. They are new every morning; great is Your faithfulness (Lamentations 3:19-23).

P. S. You may want to get another book I've written that is similar to this one: *How to Profit from Our Afflictions*, at

http://www.footstoolpublications.com/AdPages/How_to_Profit.htm
or just go to www.ftstl.com and click on "Specials".

## POSTSCRIPT

As of May 2012, I've developed fibromyalgia in my hands and feet, with much pain and little success in a cure, so far. Please pray that I'll get over this, or at least that His grace will be sufficient.

(I write this in January 2013.)

Curtis Crenshaw